GUARDING *the* HEART

A GUIDEBOOK
OF CONTEMPLATIVE
PRAYER PRACTICES

MICHAEL CONNELL

MISSION POINT PRESS

ISBN: 978-1-943995-49-3

Library of Congress Control Number: 2017918838

Cover image: "Snow Scene" by Bruce Crane
(George A. Hearn Fund, 1968; Metropolitan Museum of Art)

Published by Mission Point Press
2554 Chandler Road, Traverse City, Michigan

Printed in the United States of America.

For information on bulk purchases of this book, please contact
Mission Point Press Distribution Services at 231-421-9513
or doug.missionpointpress@gmail.com.

To Miki, my in-house editor and life partner.
And to the good sisters and staff at the
Grand Rapids Dominican Center. This book
would not have been written was it not for
their training and influence on my spiritual life
over the past 12 years.

TABLE OF CONTENTS

A Psalm of Praise

Today, Father, this blue sky lauds you.
The delicate green and orange flowers of the tulip
      poplar trees praise you.
The distant blue hills praise you,
together with the sweet-smelling air that
      is full of brilliant light.
The bickering flycatchers praise you
With the lowing cattle and the quails that
      whistle over there.
I too, Father, praise You, with all these my brothers
      and sisters,
and they give voice to my own heart
      and to my own silence.
We are all one silence, and a diversity of voices.

You have made us together,
you have made us one and many,
you have placed me here in the midst
as witness, as awareness, and as joy.

Here I am.
In me the world is present,
And you are present.
I am a link in the chain of light and of presence.
You have made me a kind of center,
But a center that is nowhere.
And yet also I am "here."

Adapted from Thomas Merton, *Conjectures of a Guilty Bystander*

Foreword

Guarding The Heart: A Guidebook of Contemplative Prayer Practices is designed for people who are on the journey and want to experience more from their prayer life. There are some of you who don't have a regular prayer life, and others who set aside time every day for prayer. And still others in between. Whatever the circumstance, there is a strong sense of being drawn by the Spirit towards a deeper way to enrich one's contact with one's Source and strengthen that relationship even more. I hope that this guide will provide some simple and powerful practices you can experiment with to begin that deeper descent into the Divine.

There are many wonderful books on prayer, from Thomas Merton to Joyce Rupp to Father Richard Rohr, David Benning, and Thomas Keating. A bibliography listing many of these excellent teachers is provided in the back of the guidebook. Many of these great books often provide some appendix or end-of-chapter examples of prayer techniques and contemplative practices. This guidebook attempts to bring all of these and many other practices together in one single volume.

The contents of this guidebook are not meant to be all-inclusive. There are hundreds of practices from all the great religions with many variations within those prayer techniques. The focus of this guidebook is on Christian prayer practices. However, selections from other faith traditions are included. An attempt is made to merge some of the practices from across traditions. For example, the powerful practice of Metta or Loving Kindness from the Buddhist tradition are introduced, along with a subtle infusion of the Christian prayer practices.

The practices are introduced in no particular order of importance. There will be a page or two of explanation that by no means should be interpreted as the definitive way to practice the technique. As stated above, these practices are provided as a simple introduction. If one resonates with you, then you are encouraged to pursue it in more depth. For example, Centering Prayer is introduced in the guidebook. There are many wonderful books, classes, and web sites that will help you further your understanding of this profound contemplative prayer practice. This introduction is just that — an introduction. The explanation of the practice will often contain my own experience with the practice either in personal prayer or in groups that I have facilitated.

Before the practices are introduced, I present a discussion on prayer in general. It covers the more practical aspects of a prayer practice, such as scheduling a time for your prayer, and the general practices you will be including. Also, there is discussion about the importance of finding a place where you will not be interrupted or distracted. These are provided as guidelines and should be used as you find them helpful.

Following these guidelines, there is a discussion of the general concepts around contemplation and contemplative prayer. Quotes from Merton, Rohr, Keating, Nouwen, and other great teachers of prayer and contemplation are provided to give the reader a better understanding of what is meant by the contemplative stance, and how powerful these practices are, and can be, for the user.

Michael Connell
November 2017

How to Use this Guidebook

This guidebook is intended to be experiential. By that I mean, after reading through the various practices, choose one to try and experiment with it. Sit quietly and read through the particular practice you have chosen. Ask the Holy Spirit for guidance and support by saying your own prayer or by using one of the prayers provided in the back of the guidebook. It is always important, I believe, to demonstrate intention as you begin to pray. After reading through the material on how to do the practice, just relax into it, open your heart, and stay present. Do not be concerned about how long it is taking or if it is working in some mystical way. Try to avoid questions about whether you are doing it right. Just be present before the Spirit, and trust that the Divine is guiding and supporting you.

There is one final crucial step. Contemplative prayer is about being present before God and experiencing a deepening of your relationship. To experience that deepening, one should spend some time in silence to reflect and ponder what is happening for you. This is the last step—silence and reflection. It may mean just sitting for a few moments in silence after the prayer time. You may choose to journal some of your thoughts and experiences. Most important is the question: "What just happened?" (Note: there is a section on journaling in the guidebook.)

As you experiment with different practices, there will probably be one or two that will resonate with you. At this point, you may want to pursue the practice in more depth. Read through the bibliography in the back of the guidebook to find more information about the practice. You can access material from one of the great teachers and their books that are listed in the bibliography, or go online to the web sites. The quickest way is to simply Google the name of the prayer practice. There may be classes available online or in your community through a church, religious center/community, or college. Especially important is to share your experience with someone who you know will be supportive of your prayer practice. It might be your spiritual director, pastor or priest, or spiritual friend/companion. In my experience as a spiritual director, these discussions always have proven to be powerful and a way for you to feel supported as you travel on your faith journey.

Guarding the Heart

Let me seek, then, the gift of silence, and
poverty, and solitude, where everything
I touch is turned into a prayer:
where the sky is my prayer, the birds are my
prayer, the wind in the trees is my prayer, for
God is all in all.

Amen

Thomas Merton, *Thoughts in Solitude* (p. 92)

Chapter One: Taking a Contemplative Stance

Developing a Regular Prayer Practice

Some Practical Issues

Some Thoughts on Contemplation

Developing a Regular Prayer Practice

When you pray, go to your inner room, close the door
and pray to your Father in secret.

The New American Bible, Matthew 6:6

Matthew 6 is a wonderful piece of scripture — Jesus teaching the apostles how to pray. Imagine the apostles listening to every word as Jesus teaches them the *Our Father*. Just before that moment, He clearly describes the practice of prayer that captures the essence of prayer and contemplation as the words above so beautifully describe. Let's take a deeper look at what Jesus was instructing the apostles and all of us to do as He describes in a very straightforward way how to pray.

When you pray: Notice that in Matthew 6:6, Jesus seems to be suggesting it is not an option to pray or not to pray. He seems to be implying that it is going to happen, and it needs to happen, and when it does this is what you need to do. I think of this as intention and making time for prayer. As you begin your prayer time, sit quietly and let God know you are there to pray, and are hoping for guidance and support in that prayer. This is a sacred time, and it is important that there is an established intention to be with the Holy Spirit. Then open your heart and be present to this profound moment.

For example, to begin your time in prayer, find a prayer you are familiar with or write one yourself (a wonderful practice that is discussed later in the guidebook). Here is one of my favorites from the Unity Church that I have been saying every morning for many years as I begin my prayer time:

One with You Dear God, I am united with all creation
in this sacred moment of prayer. I open my heart
in faith to You and to Your infinite blessings.

Go to your inner room: Jesus could not be clearer. In the practice of contemplative prayer, the obvious objective and most important aspect is the idea that this is inner work and interior reflection. We are going in and down. There is a distinct descent into our hearts. There is silence and stillness in a place where we can rest in God. This is a relationship, and we are in a two-way conversation. Inner work can be scary, and many people don't want to go there. Or they go there for a time, and get stuck and cannot go any deeper. This is where assistance from a friend, spiritual director, or clergy can help. On the spiritual journey, prayer is essential and is the tool we must access to go deeper. Transformation only happens when we go deeper, beneath the surface where God is waiting for us. Ask yourself: Am I still on the surface?

Matthew 6 also reminds us of another important aspect of our time in prayer. The homes in Jesus's time probably did not have rooms to go to, but we certainly do. In other words, go to your inner room physically as well. Find a space in your home that is designated as the place you go to pray. Let family members know that this is the room and ask that, when you go there to pray, you are not disturbed. Also, there are things you can do to make it a more sacred place. You can burn a candle as I do every morning. I also have a small table I use as an altar. You can place special items on the altar, like medals or a rosary or a crucifix. I have a small statue of St. Francis and several items I have received as gifts. Pictures of family or friends are also nice things to have on the altar.

Close the door: Again, I think Jesus is very clear here. An important aspect of any prayer time is the removal of any distractions. Turn off your devices: no cell phones or computers or TV playing in the background. As mentioned above, let people know you are in prayer, and you do not want to be disturbed. This can also refer to distracting thoughts. Remember that you are there to pray. This is why a crucial part of the time in prayer is spent in stillness and meditation. This important discipline helps you let go and surrender and be present to God.

Pray to your Father in secret: There are probably many different interpretations of this phrase. The important message for me is simply, "pray to your Father." In other words, have a conversation with God with the desire and expectation that you are deepening your relationship with Him. That is what this is all about.

Some Practical Issues to Think About as You Develop Your Prayer Practice

Making time: Briefly mentioned previously is the aspect of making time for your prayer. Sister Joyce Rupp, in her wonderful book on prayer titled *Prayer* (see bibliography), makes a strong case for setting aside time for your prayer even if it means putting it in your planner or on your electronic calendar. As a spiritual director, I have had many people tell me they have trouble finding the time to pray in their busy schedule. I tell them there are several things that are important to do in this case. First, discern through prayer if this is a discipline and regular practice you want to develop. If the answer is yes, then set aside time for it. If the answer is no, then let it go and move on. There may be a time in the future where you will be drawn to start a regular practice. The Holy Spirit is very patient.

In setting aside time, simply decide how much time each week you want to designate for prayer — one hour, two hours, etc. Then determine how many days a week — every day, every other day, etc. Now divide the time by the days to determine how much time each day you want to devote to a prayer practice. In this example, one hour a week divided by four days is fifteen minutes a day. That does not sound like much, but it is a start. Now set the time. Morning is always good as a way to start your day, but many people prefer to pray in the evening before bed.

Experiment with different prayer practices: There are many different ways to pray. Many different practices are described in this guidebook. There are also many excellent books available that provide descriptions of different prayer practices and methods of contemplation. I mentioned Joyce Rupp's book called *Prayer*. There is also David Benner, Father Richard Rohr, Tilden Edwards, and Father Thomas Keating, among others (see bibliography). The important thing is to try different practices and, if you find one that resonates with you, develop the practice and work it into your prayer life. For example, you might try reading scripture and meditating on the words (Lectio Divina) or journaling after spending time in silence. You can incorporate prayers as you come across them that resonate with you. You can try writing your own prayers, a practice I discuss later in the guidebook. I have written a number of prayers over the years, some that I still say each day:

Dear God, thank You for this day, for Your love
and understanding, Your caring and compassion,
Your goodness and Your grace, Your peace and
Your patience, Your mercy and Your forgiveness,
and Your wisdom and loving embrace. Thank You
for all these fruits of Spirit and for bringing them
into my life each day.

Be present: The simplest and the most profound aspect of prayer and contemplation is this practice of presence. God is in the presence. That is where you will meet Him. If you are off thinking about what happened at work yesterday or what you are going to discuss or present at a meeting later in the day, you are not present. Again, this is where introducing a meditation practice into your prayer life is so important. The disciplined practice of silence and meditation helps you stay in the moment. This practice will lend itself to every aspect of your day. As you sit with someone, you listen and you are present to them. You are not thinking of the next thing you are going to say. And most importantly, it increases your awareness in the moment. As you practice presence, your awareness increases, which opens you up to what God is saying to you.

Make this your time: When people tell me they are having trouble making time for prayer, I remind them of how hard they work and all the things they do for others, all of the time they spend with family, and all the responsibilities they have. I tell them they should take some time for prayer and reflection for themselves. Rather than looking at it as an obligation, consider it time that you have earned for yourself to develop yourself, and practice ways to know yourself better through reflection and peaceful stillness.

Holy Spirit, take me to the place where God is, deep in the stillness.

Some Thoughts on Prayer and Contemplation from the Great Teachers from the Past and the Present

I consider myself a seeker on the contemplative journey. I find my time in silence and prayer to be powerful and profound. For many years, I have studied the mystics and the saints to learn more about the contemplative experience. I have experimented with different practices, from the Christian tradition to the Eastern traditions. I have taught and facilitated contemplative prayer groups. For my personal prayer life, I have settled on several practices that resonate with me. I am sure that will change over time as my journey continues. I know what prayer and contemplation means for me and my own sense of how I would define it from my personal experiences. But for this guidebook, I think it would serve the reader best to let the great teachers from the past and the present help us by sharing their thoughts on prayer and contemplation.

Before I do that, I want to share a personal story. Several years ago, I was a volunteer at a food pantry. At the pantry there was a part-time chaplain who was a Catholic priest from the Eastern Orthodox Church. One day I sat with him, and we talked about my experiences at the pantry. He asked me why I volunteered. I told him I was someone who was more comfortable with the contemplative side of my spiritual life, and I had a strong sense that I needed to be more balanced and incorporate more action with that contemplation. I told him I felt, by working at the pantry, I could accomplish some of that "out of my comfort zone" action. He recognized from what I was saying that I had compartmentalized my experiences and my spiritual life into contemplation on the one side and action on the other. I will never forget what he said. "Mike, they are not separate. When you work with a client out in the lobby, you bring with you in that moment that contemplative and prayerful way about you to that encounter." This was an important insight that I have carried with me ever since.

And now, what follows are excerpts from some of the giants in contemplative teaching and practice from the past and present. Spend some time with these readings, and allow their words to inspire and motivate you.

Thomas Merton
New Seeds of Contemplation

> Contemplation is the highest expression of a man's intellectual and spiritual life. It is that life itself, fully awake, fully active, fully aware that it is alive. It is spiritual wonder. It is spontaneous awe at the sacredness of life, of being. It is gratitude for life, for awareness and for being. It is the vivid realization of the fact that life and being in us proceed from an invisible, transcendent and infinitely abundant Source. Contemplation is, above all, awareness of the reality of that Source. (p. 1)

Father Thomas Keating
The Contemplative Outreach News

> Gratitude, self-surrender, enjoyment of the Divine presence — these are the dispositions that make you contemplative. The experience of God's presence and action within you leads to a greater and greater capacity to see this action in everybody else and throughout the cosmos. It creates a marvelous open-mindedness toward all the truth. God then has the freedom to enrich you as he wills and as he has planned in incredible detail. (December 2013, web)

Henri Nouwen
Clowning In Rome: Reflections on Solitude, Celibacy,
Prayer, and Contemplation

The practice of contemplative prayer is the discipline by
which we begin to see God in our heart. It is a careful
attentiveness to him who dwells in the center of our being
such that, through the recognition of his presence we allow
him to take possession of all our senses. Through the
discipline of prayer we awaken ourselves to the God in us
and let him enter into our heartbeat and our breathing, into
our thoughts and emotions, our hearing, seeing, touching,
and tasting. It is by being awake to this God in us that we
can see him in the world around us. The great mystery of
the contemplative life is not that we see God in the world,
but that God within us recognizes God in the world. God
speaks to God, Spirit speaks to Spirit, heart speaks to heart.
Contemplation, therefore, is a participation in this divine self
recognition. It is the divine Spirit praying in us who makes
our world transparent and opens our eyes to the presence of
the divine Spirit in all that surrounds us. It is with our heart
of hearts that we see the heart of the world.
(pp. 103–104)

To know God in the world requires knowing him by heart.
To know God by heart is the purpose of a contemplative
discipline. It is a very hard discipline, especially for those of
us who are ministry "heady" people. But if we are serious
about the task of prayer, we must be willing to engage in the
tough and often agonizing struggle to break through all our
mental defenses and know our God by heart. (pp. 104–105)

Father Richard Rohr
Yes, And . . . : Daily Meditations

I try to teach people an entirely new way of knowing the world, a way of knowing that has the power to move them beyond mere ideology and dualistic thinking. We call it contemplation. Mature religion will always lead us to some form of prayer, meditation, or contemplation to balance out our daily calculating mind. Believe me, it is major surgery, and you must practice it for years to begin to rewire your egocentric responses. Contemplation is work, so much so that most give up after their first futile attempts. But the goal is not success at all, only the practice itself. The only people who pray well are those who keep trying to pray.

Such seeing — and that is what it is — gives us the capacity to be happy and happily alone, rooted in God, comfortable with paradox and mystery, and largely immune to mass consciousness and its false promises. It is called wisdom seeing, and it is the job of the elders to pass this on to the next generation. (p. 407)

Martin Laird, O.S.A

A Sunlit Absence: Silence, Awareness, and Contemplation

The practice of contemplation is one of the great spiritual arts. Not a technique but a skill, it harnesses the winds of grace that lead us out into the liberating sea of Silence. To navigate this ancient way of prayer is to put out into the deep and let down our nets for a catch (Luke 5:4). Paradoxically we discover that it is we ourselves who are caught and held in this net, an ocean-depth of moment. We realize to our great delight that the knotted netting of our anguished sense of separation from God is already immersed in these waters, where we are cleansed and freshened by its salt indeed "seasoned with salt," as St. Augustine puts it. (p. 1)

Therefore, stay awake! For you do not know
on which day your Lord will come.

Matthew 25: 42

"Awareness is a spiritual method which ... practiced
over a long period, completely frees us
with God's help from compulsive thoughts."
It "activates" the soul, enabling us "to penetrate the
Divine and hidden mysteries," and "leads us,
insofar as this is possible, to a sure knowledge
of the inapprehensible God."

Desert Father Saint Hesychios
From Laird, *A Sunlit Absence* (p. 63)

Chapter Two: Developing Awareness

The Present Moment

A Body Awareness Meditation

Practicing Presence

The Present Moment

As we begin our journey through the prayer practices in this guidebook, there is one very important spiritual truth I want to stress. The Spirit is with us and she is with us always. The problem we have is that our minds and ego selves want to take us into the future or back to the past as we attempt to pray and meditate and constantly allow ourselves to be distracted. As the mystics will tell you, God is not in those places, He is here now in the moment, the present moment. To notice and hear what God is saying to us, we must be present, focused, and approach this time of sacred conversation with great intention.

If we want a deeper relationship with God, we must work hard at developing that relationship. In any prayer practice, we are hoping for a two-way conversation. If we are off somewhere in our minds and not present to Him, there is no conversation. I cannot stress this point enough, and I am sure you are going to get tired of me reminding you of it as we move forward in the guidebook.

From the great teachers from the Eastern traditions, who gave us the powerful practices of meditation and mindfulness, to the Christian meditation practices of the Desert Fathers and Mothers, the common theme through all of their teachings is the idea of staying in the present moment. One learns this stance through the practice of stillness and contemplation. Jean-Pierre De Caussade, a French Jesuit (1675–1751), wrote what many consider the ultimate treatise from a Christian perspective on the present moment. In his book, *Abandonment to Divine Providence*, he states the following:

> Whether it be meditation, contemplation, vocal prayer, interior silence, or the active use of any of the faculties, either sensible and distinct, or almost imperceptible; quiet retreat, or active employment, whatever it may be in itself, even if very desirable, that which God wills for the present moment is best and all else must be regarded by the soul as being nothing at all. (p. 23)

Father Richard Rohr quotes from De Caussade in one of his online daily meditations. Father Richard states: "perhaps a summary sentence in his (De Caussade) teaching is this":

> If we have abandoned ourselves to God, there is only one rule for us: the duty of the present moment. What does this moment ask of me? (Center for Action and Contemplation website, Sunday, December 7, 2014)

On the next page is an example of a prayer to say as you begin the practices that follow on the coming pages. Other prayers are offered throughout the guidebook and at the end of the book.

As I Sit Here

*As I sit here, I dwell for a moment on Your life-giving
presence, right here, right now. The beating of my heart,
the ebb and flow of my breathing, and the movement of
my mind are all signs of Your ongoing presence within me.*

*As I sit here, I pause for a moment and become aware of
Your presence within me. I remind myself that there
are things you have to teach me yet, and I ask for the Grace
to hear them and let them change me.*

*As I sit here, I feel Your presence breathing life into me
and everything around me. Please help me to rise above
the noise, the noise that separates, the noise that isolates,
and to listen to your loving voice saying "come to me you
who are overburdened and I will give you rest, for I am
gentle and humble of heart."*

*As I sit here, take me to the place where I know You are,
deep in the stillness.*

Adapted from the words of the Irish Jesuits from their publication
Sacred Space, the Prayer Book, 2016. (p. 156)

A Body Awareness Meditation

From his book, *Sadhana, A Way to God*, Anthony de Mello, Jesuit priest and spiritual teacher, presents an exercise of relaxing mind and body. As a way to begin your contemplative practice, he introduces this exercise on how to relax the body and mind through use of the senses. As part of his introduction, he states:

> A word about getting out of your head: The head is not a very good place for prayer. It is not a bad place for *starting* your prayer. But if your prayer stays there too long and doesn't move into the heart, it will gradually dry up and prove tiresome and frustrating. You must learn to move out of the area of thinking and talking and move into the area of feeling, sensing, loving, and intuiting. That is the area where contemplation is born and prayer becomes a transforming power and a source of never-ending delight and peace. (p. 17)

Father de Mello talks of the importance of moving out of one's head as we sit and pray and move into the present moment, where God is waiting. One way to do that is to sit in a comfortable posture and focus on relaxing the body, from your head to your feet. This practice will help you to begin to get a sense of stillness and presence that is so important in contemplative prayer practices. Try to begin this and every practice with a prayer of intention. Alternatively, you can simply ask the Spirit to be present with you as you begin.

Sit comfortably or lay down with your arms extended to your sides and start to focus on your body. To begin, focus on your toes and your feet, and feel them begin to relax. Then move to your ankles. Pause for a moment and allow that sensation of relaxing to happen. We are not in a hurry in this exercise. Now begin to relax your lower legs, calf muscles, and shins. Bring to mind your knees and the wonderful support they give you every day, and sense them beginning to relax. Again, pause and notice any sensations you are feeling in your lower legs and knees. Next, bring to mind your upper legs, your quadriceps and hamstring muscles, and gently sense them relaxing. Now pause and notice how relaxed your legs and feet have become. Sit and ponder what that feels like.

Now move your attention to the middle part of your body, and relax the pelvis and buttocks muscles. Move up to the lower back where often people can experience discomfort. Relax your abdomen and chest, then your upper back and shoulders. These are all areas where there can be tension. If you notice that these areas are tense, spend a few extra seconds in the area. Continue to gently relax, and try to feel the tension dissipate.

Finally, move up to your head. There are many small muscles in your face. Move to each one, from your mouth to your nose and eyes, your forehead, then to your ears, and finally to the top of your head. Now scan your whole body and just sit and be in this wonderful, relaxed state. You have just done a mini meditation without realizing it, because you have remained focused and in the present moment the whole time you have been relaxing your body. At this point, Father de Mello suggests that you scan the different parts of your body and begin to feel the sensations. Simply go randomly to different areas and notice the feelings you have. Stay with these feelings for a moment, and you will gradually discern a certain stillness in your body.

What I have described in this body awareness exercise is similar to a posture practiced in yoga called savasana. In that posture, you lie on your back, feet apart and arms extended out to your sides. During this pose, you can take yourself through the relaxation exercise I described above, going from your feet to your head. I began the practice of yoga in my late twenties. I did not realize it at the time, but, by practicing this pose, I was experiencing the beginnings of my contemplative journey of silence and stillness. I highly recommend the practice of yoga as an adjunct to the prayer practices in this guidebook.

Below is a prayer I composed from the words and thoughts of Father de Mello introduced in this section. It can be used before or after this meditation or many of the contemplative practices that follow:

Holy One, please help me as I sit here to pray.
Help me move from my head to my heart
where I know you are.

I desire my prayer life to be rich and a never-ending
source of delight and peace.

I fear if I don't move into my heart as I pray,
my prayer life will become tiresome and frustrating
and I will stop.

Teach me to bring more feeling, sensing, loving
and intuiting to my contemplative prayer practices.

Provide me with the transforming power to deepen
my prayer life and therefore deepen my relationship
with You.

Amen

Prayer adapted from the de Mello quote above from his book, *Sadhana, a Way to God.*

Practicing Presence

If you are not used to sitting in silence and simply being present, this is a very good way to start your contemplative prayer journey, because it will help you ease into the experience. Most people seem to want to avoid silence. We are so used to the noise of everyday life and seem to almost thrive on the distractions we create, we avoid the experience and actually seem to fear it. Several years ago I was helping a group of men organize a men's retreat. At the first meeting as the discussion began around the topic of what we were going to do, an older man spoke up with some amount of disdain and concern in his voice: "This isn't going to be one of those silent retreats, I hope?" It wasn't.

To begin, find a place where you will not be disturbed or distracted. Turn off any device that might distract you. Sit comfortably with your feet on the floor and your back as straight as possible. As I discussed in the introduction, it is important to start with a prayer of intention like the prayer *"As I Sit Here"* on page 21. You might, instead, find one that resonates with you from the prayers in the back of the guidebook, or you can use one you are currently using in prayer. Say the prayer out loud if you can, slowly with intent and feeling. This will help you in the process of slowing down or coming down from your daily activities.

Close your eyes and breathe normally. Become aware of your desire to be with God in His loving presence. In his wonderful book on prayer, *Opening to God*, David Benner puts it beautifully in his discussion of Centering Prayer: "This isn't the time to

think about God. It's time to simply be open to and with God."
(p. 142) Gently attempt to keep yourself in the present moment.
Concentrate on your in and out breath. As thoughts enter your
mind, and they will at an alarming rate as you first experience
this kind of practice, just let them go and come back to your
breathing. As a starting point, practice this quiet breathing for
about five or ten minutes.

An important final step after finishing the practice is to check
in with yourself. Ask yourself a few questions. How do you feel
after sitting quietly for ten minutes? Are you more relaxed, or
do you feel about the same or possibly more agitated than when
you began? Is this something you could do for more than ten
minutes, possibly as long as 20 or 30 minutes? If it was somewhat
uncomfortable, reflect on how it was uncomfortable and why.
Remember, contemplative practices are about going deeper and
attempting to know yourself better. This check-in is that kind of
practice. There will be more about this kind of reflection with the
practices that follow.

On the following page is a short prayer from Thomas Merton that
I have always found to be profound. It is a prayer I say almost
every morning. Before you begin the above practice, consider
saying this short prayer. Alternatively, consider saying it after you
have finished.

Let me seek, then, the gift of silence, and
poverty, and solitude, where everything
I touch is turned into a prayer:
where the sky is my prayer, the birds are my
prayer, the wind in the trees is my prayer, for
God is all in all.

Amen

Thomas Merton, *Thoughts in Solitude* (p. 92)

*If one ... finds in one or two words matter which
yields thought, relish, and consolation, one should not
be anxious to move forward, even if the whole hour is
consumed on what is being found.*

St. Ignatius, from his *Spiritual Exercises*

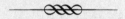

*In God's loving presence I unwind the past day,
starting from now and looking back, moment by
moment. I gather all the goodness and light, in
gratitude. I attend to the shadows and what they say
to me, seeking healing, courage and forgiveness.*

The Irish Jesuits, *Sacred Space: The Prayer Book 2016* (p. 40)

Chapter Three: From the Monastic Tradition

The Practice of Lectio Divina

The Practice of Lectio Divina in Small Groups

The Examen Prayer

The Practice of Lectio Divina (Sacred Reading)

Lectio Divina is a practice that brings a contemplative stance to the reading and study of scripture. This is not the study of scripture that a person would encounter in a Bible study group. Not to say this kind of study of the Bible is not important, but this practice of meditating on the Word is just a different approach to the encounter with scripture. It is less about trying to figure out what a passage is saying or the historical significance of the reading and more about what the Spirit is saying to you as you read the passage and reflect on it.

As a starting point, simply choose a short verse from the Bible (four to eight lines are recommended), and then prepare yourself to reflect on the Word in a deeper, more experiential way. As in other practices, it is important to prepare yourself. Sit quietly in a comfortable posture with both feet on the floor. This is a contemplative prayer practice, so those same preparation techniques are in play here. Bring a sense of intention to the practice by saying a short prayer. It can be as simple as: "Holy Spirit, I ask for your guidance and support. Please provide me with any insight you feel I need at this moment."

There are four stages in this practice of Lectio Divina: lectio, or reading; meditatio, or reflection; oratio, or response; and contemplatio, or rest. After you have selected the piece of scripture, you will be reflecting on, read it slowly, pausing between lines. If possible, say the words out loud. Now sit in silence, and ponder the words. Allow the words to wash over you. Trust that the Spirit is guiding you. After a few minutes, come back to the passage and read it again slowly. As you sit in silence again, ponder these sacred words and see if anything speaks to you; go deeper and allow the Spirit to engage you. Was there a word or phrase that resonated with you? Just let this happen. Open your heart to the Holy One. Remember, this is an exercise of the heart, not the head.

In the third reading, again read it slowly with intention and then sit in silence. For this third time, reflect on the words and see if there is a moment of insight, possibly about a particular circumstance in your life where you are looking for guidance. Don't expect a mystical experience, but you can expect something, and open your awareness to that something. This takes practice, as do all of these prayer practices, so these insights may take time to manifest themselves.

The fourth and last reading of the passage is a time for just resting in God's presence. Ruth Haley Barton, in her book, *Sacred Rhythms: Spiritual Practices that Nourish Your Soul and Transform Your Life*, describes this fourth period of silence this way:

> In this final reading you are invited to ... a place of rest in God. You have given your response its full expression, so now you can move into a time of waiting and resting in God's presence.... This is a posture of total yieldedness and abandon to the great Lover of your soul. (p. 61)

After ten to twenty minutes of contemplative sitting and resting in God, you can simply move into your day and take this gift from the Spirit with you. You may want to journal your experience — a great way to finish the time with the sacred word.

In her book *The Wisdom Jesus*, Cynthia Bourgeault, an Episcopal priest and spiritual teacher, talks about the practice of Lectio Divina. She writes the following:

> Many people feel intimidated diving into the scriptures by themselves, convinced that one must be a biblical scholar to have the authority to proceed. But this simply isn't so. For fifteen hundred years Christian monks — and now an

increasing number of lay people — have been using a practice called *lectio divina* (Latin for "sacred reading") to carry them deeper into their own heart-knowing. It's a simple yet profound way of praying the scripture that transcends mental processing in favor of a deeper form of spiritual ingestion. (p. 150)

Later in her chapter on Lectio Divina, Bourgeault presents some helpful suggestions about this practice of prayer and meditation:

Whatever catches your attention, stay with it and work with it. Bring all your imagination to bear upon it. But remember, this is not biblical research. Don't reach for the scholarly commentaries, not now anyway. This practice is not about acquiring information or learning about what the experts have to say; it is about allowing the text to break open and resonate in the authority of your own heart. (p. 153)

The prayer below is from Henri Nouwen. It is a beautiful prayer to say as you begin your Lectio practice or after you have finished:

Dear God,

Speak gently in my silence.

When the loud outer noises of my surroundings
and the loud inner noises of my fears
keep pulling me away from you,
help me to trust that you are still there
even when I am unable to hear you.

Give me ears to listen to your small, soft voice, saying:

"Come to me you who are overburdened,
and I will give you rest...
for I am gentle and humble of heart."

Let that loving voice be my guide.
Amen

From *With Open Hands*, Nouwen, p. 40

The Practice of Lectio Divina in Small Groups

Lectio Divina can also be done in small prayer groups. The process is the same as described above with some minor additions to allow for the whole group to participate. The facilitator leads the group in a prayer to begin the Lectio. This serves to bring intention to the experience and to ask for guidance and support for the participants during the meditation.

The facilitator reads the chosen reading aloud and allows for several minutes of silence so the group can simply listen and focus on the sacred words. The facilitator then reads the verse a second time. Again, after a few minutes of silence, the facilitator prompts the participants to share a word or phrase that resonated with them from the verse. Each person, in turn, voices the word or phrase that touched them. After everyone has shared their word or phrase, the leader reads the verse slowly for a third time. After some more silence, the leader prompts the group again for another word or phrase that stood out for them.

During the silence after the leader reads the selected verse, the participants are asking the Spirit to guide them to the words that speak to their hearts. Sharing these words with your fellow participants, and hearing the words others are sharing, can be a powerful experience and an important part of the practice.

The facilitator then reads the verse for a final time. At this time the facilitator can allow for ten to twenty minutes of silence and meditation. After this time of silence, the leader can then check in with the group to see if anyone wants to share any insight or meaningful thought they experienced. Any sharing is voluntary, but is always meaningful for both the person sharing and for all the participants. Once a sense of trust is developed among the members, sharing becomes much easier.

The Examen Prayer

Saint Ignatius Loyola gave us many gifts. His *Spiritual Exercises*, used primarily as a month-long guide for a thirty-day directed silent retreat, contains within it the Examen Prayer. This is a prayer of examination of the day (or week or month) reflecting on your experiences and what you noticed about yourself and your relationship with God. It contains a simple but powerful five-point exercise of reflection to be used at the end of the day that you can incorporate into your prayer practice.

The following comes from the translation of the *Spiritual Exercises* by David Fleming, SJ. In his book, *Draw Me Into Your Friendship*, Fleming translates a description of the Examen Prayer by Ignatius and the five points of reflection. Some of the text has been abbreviated:

> The method of the particular examination is nothing more than focusing on that style of prayer used for making a general examination of conscience:
>
> *Give thanks to God for all the favors received. (Gratitude)*
>
> *Ask for help of the Spirit to enlighten you so that you might see the light of God's grace. (Petition)*

*Go back over the events of the day to see where God
has been present in your life. (Review)*

*Express sorrow and ask God for forgiving love to heal
and strengthen you. (Forgiveness)*

*Pray for the grace to be more totally available to God
who loves you so totally. (Renewal) (p. 33)*

The words in parenthesis at the end of each point were added as a way of focusing each point and remembering them as you sit down to do the Examen Prayer.

Father Timothy Gallagher, O.M.V., has written extensively on the work and gifts of St. Ignatius. His book, *The Examen Prayer: Ignatian Wisdom for Our Lives Today*, explains the practice extensively, and I recommend the book for anyone who wishes to learn more about the Examen Prayer. Father Gallagher writes of his own experience with the Examen Prayer in his book this way:

As time goes by I see more and more clearly why Ignatius so warmly recommends daily examen. Examen is our way of being regularly available to God so that divine light and love can heal our darkness and point the way toward spiritual growth. So much can change when I am open *every day* to hearing God's voice in this way. (p. 35)

The Examen Prayer is intended to be a time of reflection and a prayer practice that helps you go deeper in your understanding of yourself and your relationship with God. As we have talked about, this is about relationship. In this practice, you are having a conversation with God, conversing with the Divine about your day in a prescribed way as delineated by Ignatius in the *Spiritual Exercises*. If you are praying the Examen on a daily basis, it makes the most sense to reserve some time in the evening to sit for a few minutes to review your day. But this practice can also be done in a review of the week or several weeks if the daily practice does not work well for you. The important thing is the reflection and the inner work that is required and the deepening that follows that inner work.

To begin, find a quiet place to sit and be with God. Let the thoughts of the day go, and allow yourself to be simply present to God. If you are just beginning the practice, it might help to have a card or sheet of paper handy with the five points written down. Begin with thoughts of Gratitude by reflecting back on your day and consider for what you are thankful. Invite the Spirit to be with you as you consider your day. You will be drawn to the good things that happened or the people in your life that you encountered who brought joy or happiness to your experiences. You may also want to examine the not-so-pleasant encounters you had and how you handled them. Be thankful for the teaching moment that those encounters may have given you. Remember, this is a time of reflection and examination of your inner self in a sacred effort to learn more about yourself and your relationship with God.

In the next point, think about what you may need or desire from God. This for many may be the easiest of the five points as we often, in our prayer lives, are in this posture of Petition. You might ask for insight and for grace to see the way God is working in your life. What might God be inviting me to do or become? You might use this time to ask God for healing for yourself or a loved one. You might be in need of help with a particular relationship. Always remember, in any petition of this kind, "stay awake" to what guidance or support the Spirit may offer you. If you are spending this time in prayer and asking for God's wisdom and help, it only makes sense that you need to then be aware of what help may be forthcoming.

The next step in the Examen is a Review of your actions through the day. As we encounter people and experience the many reactions, both positive and negative, in those encounters, how aware are we of those reactions. As Father Gallagher states in his book on the Examen: "Can we discern which are of God and should be followed and which are not and should be rejected." (p. 79)

Maybe we experienced anger in an encounter, or we were critical or judgmental in our reactions. Father Gallagher puts it beautifully in his book:

> In the prayer of examen we ask: Where was God in all of this today? Toward what was the Lord calling me in the day? How did I respond to this call? Were there inclinations and thoughts this day that were not of God? If there were, was I able to discern and resist them? (p. 79)

In step four we simply ask God for Forgiveness. We ponder what happened during the day and reflect on where we may have allowed our false self, as Merton would call it, or our ego self or small self, as it is called in the Buddhist tradition, to dictate our reaction to a particular situation. Again, it is important to be aware of these situations. The Examen is an opportunity to look more closely at your reactions and learn from them. Above all else, in step four, we are asking the Lord to heal us and forgive us and give us the strength to make whatever changes we see are needed in our lives to bring us closer to Him.

The final step in the Examen is Renewal. As you relate to the experiences of the day, begin this final process thinking about the future and what God may have in store for you. You may want to look to the next few days and what may be coming up in your work life or personal life and pray for right action ... that with every encounter, you are patient, tolerant, and understanding, and, as Joyce Rupp states in one of her many beautiful prayers:

Great Teacher, you draw me to your heart.
You reach me with your love.
You inspire me with your message,
and then you send me out to others.
May I love well.
As I go forth from my prayer,
may I reflect the radiance of your goodness.

Amen.

From *Prayer,* a book by Sister Joyce Rupp (p. 120)

The composition, by imagining the place.

*Here it will be to see in imagination the road
to Nazareth to Bethlehem.*

*Consider its length and breadth, whether it is level or
winds through valleys and hills.*

*Similarly, look at the place or cave of the nativity:
How big is it, or small? How low or high?*

And how is it furnished?

St. Ignatius, imagining the nativity scene,
from his *Spiritual Exercises.*

James Martin, *The Jesuit Guide to (Almost) Everything* (p. 149)

Chapter Four: Imaginative Prayer

Scripture Imaging

Developing A Prayer Group or Prayer Council

A Conversation with a Spiritual Giant

Scripture Imaging

James Martin, SJ, in his excellent book on Ignatian spirituality, *The Jesuit Guide to (Almost) Everything,* talks about the prayer practice for which St. Ignatius Loyola became so well known: imagining that you are in a particular scene from scripture. This form of contemplative prayer or imaginative prayer, as it is often called, can be a powerful spiritual practice. Martin states in his book:

> In Ignatian contemplation you "compose the place" by imagining yourself in a scene from the Bible, or in God's presence, and then taking part in it. It's a way of allowing God to speak to you through your imagination. (p. 145)

After describing the practice, Martin talks about what happens during and after:

> God desires to communicate with you all the time, but when you *intentionally* open yourself up to God's voice, you can often hear it more clearly. To use the metaphor of friendship, it is similar to saying to a friend, "You have my undivided attention." Ignatian contemplation enables us to hear more easily, or differently, and to recognize something that might otherwise be overlooked. (p. 151)

Another great book on how to use the Ignatian Spiritual Exercises and the practice of scripture imaging is the *Ignatian Workout* by Tim Muldoon. In his discussion of the process that

Ignatius called "Composition of Place," the author states that by using your imagination in this way, you can deepen your prayer practice in often very profound ways. Muldoon writes:

> By bringing imagination to bear on a particular aspect of our spiritual lives, we come to better understand what struggles we face, what issues we have yet to resolve, what ways God is calling us to grow. It is a very straightforward way of paying attention to our deeper selves, which often get overlooked in our busy lives. For while our spirituality is always underneath the layers of consciousness we use in everyday life, it often remains hidden.... The exercise of imagination in prayer makes us pay attention to our spiritual core and to the ways we manifest the character of this core in our choices. (p. 55)

In my presentation on the practice of Lectio Divina earlier in the guidebook, I talked about how that practice was different than just reading or studying scripture at an intellectual level. The practice of imaging scripture is a way of going deeper with the reading. Many of the same techniques that you would use with Lectio are in play. The idea is not just to read through a passage, but to pause and reflect and to read it slowly with intention. There are many wonderful stories and events describing Jesus's life, His experiences, and teachings that can be used in this practice.

To begin, decide on a particular scripture passage, sit quietly, close your eyes for a few moments, and ask for guidance and support. As I have emphasized in the other prayer experiences, always let the Spirit know your intention, and ask for support and insight. This can be a powerful experience if you can just let yourself relax into it. Now read the passage slowly, out loud if possible. Begin to get a sense of the story and what is happening. Sit and let the words resonate with you. You may be very familiar with the story. That is fine. Breathe deeply to relax yourself and then read the story a second time.

At this point let your imagination take over. Close your eyes and begin to picture the story as if it were happening right now. Be very specific in your imagining. Begin to see yourself in the scene and then imagine things around you. Where are you? Is it early or later in the day? What is the weather like? Is it hot, or pleasant, or cold? Are you outside or inside? Now notice the characters in the scene. Do you recognize anyone? If it is a scene with Jesus, where is He in the scene and how does He look to you? Are the apostles with him? And now most importantly, who are you in the story? Are you in the crowd or are you one of the main characters?

To get even more into the story, use your senses. Can you smell or taste anything? Does the smell have good or bad associations for you? Again, let yourself go and relax and let your imagination take you deeper into the events that are happening. I remember when I did this for the first time, I was Bartemeus, the blind man. In that event I went from not seeing anything, only hearing and feeling things, to being able to see after Jesus gave me sight. A technique I sometimes use is, after the event, I ask Jesus to sit with me and explain his perspective on what just happened. In one of my experiences, I imagined I was a reporter for the newspaper, and Jesus and I sat as I interviewed him.

Bring yourself out of the experience slowly. You can enrich the practice and bring more of a contemplative experience to the meditation by sitting in silence for ten or fifteen minutes and resting in God's presence.

After your time in silence, spend some time reflecting on what happened in the story for you. If you talked to Jesus or other characters, what was the conversation about? What did you learn from the experience about yourself? In this phase of the practice, it is very important to be open to the Spirit and the insight you are getting. The best way to do this last part of the exercise is to journal what happened and write about your experiences. If you do this in the morning as part of your prayer practice, take the story into your day and see if you notice anything that may happen during the day that brings you back to the meditation.

When you are finished, say a prayer of gratitude to the Holy Spirit for being with you and allowing you to experience the sacred moment. As in any of these contemplative practices, it takes some practice and repetition. If this exercise resonates with you after trying it, check the bibliography for the books on Ignatian spirituality I quoted above to learn more about the technique.

Developing a Prayer Group or Prayer Council

A number of years ago, as part of my morning prayer ritual, I began a practice of imagining that I was being accompanied in my prayer session by a small prayer group. They have been with me ever since. I started with a small number of just three or four, adding a few over the years and removing a few. The group is comprised of saints and icons and friends who are now deceased. When I begin my prayer time, I close my eyes and sit quietly for a few moments. Then I call them together with the words: "Let us pray. I ask my prayer group to gather."

I make it a point to greet each one with a personal greeting. Sometimes I imagine embracing them or shaking their hands or just acknowledging them. For me the composition of the group was easy to imagine. I begin with Jesus. He acts as the leader and, after I have greeted everyone, I imagine Jesus saying to all present, "Let us pray." There is St. Francis, who is sitting with a more recent addition, Clare. I then greet my guardian angel and usually thank her for watching over my family and me. Thomas Merton is next and is often sitting at a table reading. After Merton, I move on to Mary and Joseph.

The remaining members of the group are my old and dear friend, Andy, from childhood, and, of course, I include the Holy Spirit. Additionally, there is an old friend and lifetime spiritual companion, my sister-in-law Denise, who died of cancer several years ago.

After Jesus makes the declaration of "Let us pray," I begin my prayer ritual. The group, at this point, moves to the background and is no longer directly in my consciousness, but I feel their presence as I move forward in prayer. At the end of my Centering Prayer meditation, I bring the group back into my consciousness and say goodbye to each one and thank them for being with me.

In my title, above, I use the word "council" along with group. The reason for that is I often use my time with the prayer group to have a short dialogue with one or more of the members. For example, as I have been writing this guidebook, I always thank Thomas Merton, one of the great spiritual writers of the twentieth century, for guidance and support, and for ideas and inspiration for my writing. In issues around family, I sometimes will sit with Mary and Joseph for a few moments and share something that may be going on in the family, and ask for guidance and support. I believe if there is an issue on my mind, there is always someone in the group who can help.

I will always remember a few years ago a session with my spiritual director. I shared with him a particular problem I was experiencing. Recalling I had told him of my use of this technique of a prayer group, he suggested I talk to Jesus about the issue at the next gathering of the group.

To develop your own prayer group, sit quietly with intention and ask the Spirit to guide and support your efforts to assemble a group to accompany you during your daily prayer time. As with other imaging I have presented in the guidebook, let this happen naturally without forcing it. Let the place you are gathering form in your mind. It might be the kitchen table, or it might be outside in the garden, or on the porch or deck of your home. It may also be a more sacred setting like a church, possibly a sacred place you have visited that means a lot to you.

Now imagine someone joining you. Identify the person, and greet them and thank them for being with you. The figure you see may not be totally clear in your mind's eye, but you will know who it is. Invite the person to sit with you. Now wait for a second entity to join you and do the same. How many come in to join you will be part of the natural unfolding of the process. Be sure to greet each entity and thank them for their presence.

After you sense you have everyone together, go around to each one and ask them if they have anything they would like to tell you. This can be a very powerful and profound experience. Just relax and open your heart to what is being said to you. After you have talked to everyone, thank each one for being with you. You can take the opportunity to speak specifically to one of the entities and ask a question or give thanks for something that you believe may have helped in your life. As I mentioned above, I sometimes thank my guardian angel for helping to keep myself and members of my family safe and well.

After your imaging, it is important to journal your experience, and note the location of the meeting and the members of the group and what they may have said to you. This will help you remember the images the next time you gather the prayer group. If this becomes a regular practice, the size of the group may change and the membership may change as well. Always remember to allow the Holy Spirit to guide you in the process.

A Conversation with a Spiritual Giant

A very powerful contemplative practice similar to the Ignatian practice of scripture imaging is the practice of meeting with and having a conversation with a Spiritual Giant or icon such as Jesus, or St. Francis, or Mary. Who you choose for your giant is up to you, and in most cases, it does not take long to think of who that might be. In my formation training to become a spiritual director, it was required that we choose a Spiritual Giant to accompany us on our two-year journey. We made presentations about them and their prayer life and theology. My choice was easy, because St. Francis had been with me for many years, and I already felt a close relationship with this great saint.

Choosing a Spiritual Giant is not necessary to do the imaging exercise, but it can enhance the experience if you spend some time discerning who that might be and reading about him/her. If you are going to have a conversation with a friend, it can only help if you get to know them. The most obvious choice is Jesus, and He is probably a good icon with whom to start. If you have already done some scripture imaging, you may have already experienced having a conversation with Him. This is a good time for you to use a journal to capture the main focus of your conversation afterward.

This practice requires a quiet place where you will not be interrupted. Sit comfortably, close your eyes, and center yourself, focusing on the present moment. As with other practices, ask the Holy Spirit for guidance and support, and for any insight that may be gained from the encounter. Relax your body and breath easily. In your imagination, picture in your mind a peaceful place in nature that you are familiar with or somewhere totally new. As you are walking, you come upon an overlook, and there is a bench. You sit down and gaze out over the beautiful landscape. What does it look like? What do you see? What time of day is it? Notice if there is a breeze and the temperature.

After a few moments, you sense someone is with you. You turn and standing behind you is Jesus. He smiles and greets you. You stand and approach Him, and he reaches out his hand and places it on your shoulder and says, "Michael, it is good to see you." You then sit together on the bench and look over the landscape together. After a few moments, He asks you if there is anything you would like to ask Him. This is an important moment, so allow the Spirit to work with you and ask whatever comes to mind. You could ask about a problem you are having or a decision you are working through. What is His response? Again, simply allow for whatever comes to you.

After the exchange about your question, He tells you there is something He would like to tell you. What does He say to you? What is your response? After a few moments of silence, He stands and you stand with Him. He smiles and you embrace. He then walks down the path and out of sight. You sit back down and ponder the encounter for a few moments. You then stand and begin walking down the path yourself, and you bring yourself back to the room and space where you were. This can be a powerful experience. After finishing the imaging, sit in silence for ten or fifteen minutes and simply rest in God's presence.

You can continue the practice as often as you like. You can change the location or simply use the same one. The conversation can be about anything that comes to you. Simply allow the Holy Spirit to work with you and accept whatever comes to mind. Thank your Spiritual Giant for the experience and whatever insight you may have gained. Also, it is always helpful, and can enrich the experience, if you take some time to journal.

Several years ago, I had the good fortune to visit Assisi in Italy with my family. We visited all the famous landmarks inside and outside the city where St. Francis lived and preached. Just outside of Assisi is the little church, San Damiano, where Francis had the encounter with Jesus as he stared at the cross on the altar. Now whenever I imagine having a conversation with Francis, and we have had many, I always imagine us on a bench in front of the small church in Assisi.

Bless to us, O God,

the moon that is above us,

the earth that is beneath us,

the friends who are around us,

Your image deep within us.

Amen

From the *Iona Abbey Worship Book* (p.134)

Chapter Five: Praying for Others

Praying For Others

The Blessing Prayer

The Practice of Tonglen

The Practice of Metta or Loving Kindness

Praying for Others

There are two questions that seekers have been asking since the beginning of religious prayer practice and the spiritual journey: Is God listening when I pray? Does He hear my prayers and really answer them? Obviously, many believe that He does. But there is always that uncertainty that requires a strong faith to endure. I am sometimes surprised when I ask people about their prayer life, and they struggle with the idea of praying for others, especially people with whom they are close. I personally pray for my family and friends every day. Frankly, I can't imagine sitting down to pray and not saying a prayer for the important people in my life.

In my spiritual-direction practice, the person I am meeting with (often referred to as a directee) sometimes questions whether God is listening to his or her prayers and if prayer really works. When I ask someone who is struggling with a particular person if he or she ever prays for this person, the puzzled look I get is very telling. Once in a while I ask the directee to say a prayer for the person at that moment, spontaneously. This often can be a wonderful moment.

The following three prayer practices from the Christian and Buddhist traditions are practices that focus on praying for others. Do I believe that praying for others actually works, and God is really listening? Yes, I do. More important than just believing it works, I have faith it works and it is, in fact, helping in some way. Sister Joyce Rupp, in her must-read book on prayer called *Prayer*, states:

> The longer we pray, the more we realize prayer is bigger than we are, more expansive and deeper. When we least expect it, our prayer brings us into further clarity about who we are and how we are to be with God and the world. These experiences encourage us to lessen our stronghold on wanting to control, to know and have proof. Unexpected graced moments in prayer restore our confidence in the process and help us to trust our intention to become more loving. These little glimpses encourage us to give ourselves to what we believe to be of most value. We leave the *finished product* of prayer to the One who knows the longings of our heart. (p. 11)

When I was in formation training for certification in spiritual direction, I met a retired priest who often visited some of the classes. I spent some time with him in conversation concerning my decisions about becoming a spiritual director. He was a deeply spiritual man and, as I found out later, a well known spiritual director. One evening when we finished our time together and he affirmed my intention to become a director, he put his hand on my shoulder and said: "I will put you in the barrel." He was referring to his prayer barrel containing all of those he was praying for at the time. Father Fritz was a man of great faith, and I felt honored to be in his prayer barrel.

The Blessing Prayer

On Sunday mornings in churches around the world, there is a part of the service where a person from the congregation stands at the pulpit and reads a litany of people's names and events in the form of a petition for God's help. This is a time when the entire church has the opportunity to pray together for particular persons from the parish or a world event or cause. After the name of each person or event is read, the congregation responds, "Lord, hear our prayer." The Blessing Prayer is a personal form of that practice, which can be done on your own. This is a time to see what is in your barrel, and who else you may want to put in that barrel.

Sit quietly and with intention. Bring to mind a particular person with whom you are close to — it may be a spouse or a child or dear friend or parent. Ask that the person be blessed and always say his/her name. You can add to that petition anything you may want to emphasize about the person. If the individual is struggling with an illness or a difficult problem, you can request that the Spirit provide guidance and support during this difficult time. The person may be traveling, for which you can request safety. Now broaden your list to others in your family circle and ask for them to be blessed. As you continue this practice and add it to your prayer list, it will get longer and longer. It is important to include people you may be struggling with at the time. This will help you develop a sense of compassion for the person even though it is challenging to do so.

I have been doing the Blessing Prayer practice for many years. It includes all of my family and friends, my colleagues in spiritual direction, all the children in my life, and the children who are suffering around the world. I ask that they all be cared for and nourished. I pray for the homeless and the wonderful people who help them in churches and food pantries. I added all of the wonderful spiritual and medical caregivers in hospice programs. I personally experienced their compassionate care as I watched them caring for a friend several years ago. I provide you with these examples as a way to prompt you to consider who you may want to include on your list.

As a final prayer after you have listed all those in a particular category, you can add a general blessing. For example, after I have finished asking for blessings for all my family members, I say the following:

May they all be blessed. May they all be filled with joy, happiness, love, and light. May they be healthy and safe. Guide and support them in their spiritual journey and help them to experience their True Selves and help them deepen their relationship with You.

The Practice of Tonglen

Awakening the Compassion Within

The Buddhist tradition has introduced the world to many beautiful prayer practices. Tonglen is one of those practices. It is a way of praying for others that awakens a sense of compassion and a deeper sense of the suffering in an individual or group. The idea behind the prayer practice is to literally take on the suffering of a person we know to be hurting and who we wish to help. It is a way of holding the suffering of another and, in the process, awakening the compassion within our own hearts that is deeply rooted in our soul and longing to come out. It is like that moment when you are watching a story on TV, or reading a story on the internet or in the newspaper, and you are moved to tears. That is that same compassion within you coming out.

The first step in the practice of Tonglen is to prepare yourself for it. As with the other prayer practices, sit quietly and with intention. Bring to mind the Holy Spirit, and ask for guidance and support. Say a short prayer and open your heart to that compassion within you. You might want to imagine a presence of an icon sitting with you like Jesus or one of the saints to assist you in the prayer. Remember to always thank them for their presence.

After a few moments of silence, begin to notice the in-and-out rhythm of your breathing. You can use a simple visualization.

As you inhale, imagine you are inhaling some negativity, or polluted or dark thought. As you exhale, imagine you are releasing this negativity and breathing out pure, bright, nourishing air. Establish this movement of accepting and releasing or sending out with each breath.

The next stage of the prayer is the main focus of the session. Bring to mind those who you wish to be the recipients of your prayer, including yourself. You can prepare the list ahead of time or simply allow the guidance of Spirit to provide the names for you. This could be an individual or a group of people. It may be a child who is ill or going through a difficult time at school, or a spouse or friend who is suffering from a chronic illness or recovering from surgery. It could be the refugees from the war in the Middle East or the Native Americans in the Southwest who are suffering from a lack of clean water.

Now bring to mind a specific person or group and their trauma or struggle. With each inhalation accept their difficulty, and with each exhalation send to them whatever you sense might help their situation. If you have trouble with this, just imagine sending them healing light. Spend a few minutes with this rhythmic breathing and stay present. If your mind wanders, gently bring it back to the prayer and the person for whom you are praying. After a specific time with an individual or group, begin to expand outward to all people or groups that come to mind who may be in similar circumstances, beyond just people in your neighborhood or church community.

Close by breathing out, letting any tension or pain that arose in the prayer dissolve as you exhale. Relax your body and simply breath deeply. Sit quietly for ten or twenty minutes and simply rest in God's presence. Finish the session thanking the Spirit for being with you as well as any icon you imagined being with you during the Tonglen practice.

(Some of the descriptions of how to practice Tonglen were adapted from an article written by Ethan Nichtern in the *Shambhala Sun* magazine, July 2014.)

The Practice of Metta or Loving Kindness

Metta (or the loving kindness meditation) is a wonderful Buddhist prayer practice using a set of phrases directed at ourselves and others. These phrases foster a sense of love and kindness and compassion, and open our hearts to ourselves and the people in our lives. Sharon Salzberg, in her book, *Loving-Kindness: The Revolutionary Art of Happiness*, says of the practice of metta:

> Metta is a priceless treasure that enlivens us and brings us into an intimacy with ourselves and others. It is the force of love that will lead beyond fragmentation, loneliness, and fear. (p. 45)

In a wonderful little book called *The Gift of Loving Kindness* by Mary Brantley and Tesilya Hanauer, the authors describe the practice this way:

> The simplest explanation of loving-kindness meditation is that you repeat a series of phrases aimed at yourself, a loved one, a person you feel neutral about, a difficult person, and, finally, all living things with the intention of generating great friendliness for yourself and others. (p. 2)

To begin the practice, sit quietly and with intention. Ask the Holy Spirit to be with you as you are about to pray for yourself and others in your life. Center yourself, relaxing your body and mind, breathing evenly and being present to the movements of the Spirit. You will be directing phrases at yourself and at other individuals or groups. There are many different phases you can use, and I will present some examples at the end. The most commonly used phrases are as follows:

May I be happy.
May I be healthy.
May I be at peace.
May I be safe.

After directing the phrases at yourself, you then bring to mind a person with whom you are very close. It could be your spouse, a child, parent, or friend. You then repeat the four phrases inserting their name: "May Michelle be happy, May she be healthy: May she be at peace: May she be safe." You then move to the next person in the sequence. It can be a person you are neutral about, the store clerk from this afternoon, or a person at work, and you repeat the same four phrases. May this person be happy, healthy, at peace, and safe.

Now it can get a bit more challenging as you bring to mind a difficult person in your life. It could be someone who is good at pushing your buttons and you just have trouble liking. It may be a grumpy colleague or a friend who can sometimes get on your nerves. Bring them to mind and repeat the phrases. After a few moments, finish the meditation by bringing to mind a group. Some people use the thought of sending metta to all creatures on earth or to all sentient beings. You can also bring to mind a particular community or congregation or large group of friends or an organization.

Another way to practice metta is to use an icon to assist you. Imagine you are sitting in a room and Jesus or Mary or St. Francis, or some other saint or spiritual giant that has had an influence on you, enters the room and sits with you. Imagine this icon greeting you and then looking into your eyes and repeating the four phrases: "Michael, may you be happy, may you be healthy, may you be at peace, may you be safe."

Then the person with whom you are very close enters the

room and sits down, and the icon repeats the four phrases to that person. This is followed by the neutral person and so on. As a final thought, you can imagine standing with this icon on a hillside, and looking over the earth and repeating the phrases for all of God's creatures.

After your time in this sacred practice, spend fifteen or twenty minutes in silence, simply resting in God. Metta is a powerful prayer practice. Bringing this final contemplative silence to the practice can make it even more meaningful.

If the practice of metta resonates with you, I encourage you to get copies of the books I mentioned above or simply google "metta practice" or "loving-kindness meditation," and you will find some helpful material to get started and go deeper into the practice. Below are some suggested phrases you can use as you further your practice. And of course you can also compose your own phrases. The phrases provided below were taken from *The Gift of Loving Kindness* and *A Woman of Wisdom: Honoring and Celebrating Who We Are,* by Caroline Joy Adams.

May I be free from worry.
May I be well.
May I be patient.
May I be filled with compassion.
May I enjoy the moment.
May I be calm and at peace.
May I be filled with loving-kindness.
May I accept myself just as I am.
May I be free from pain and suffering.
May my heart remain open.
May my spirit be light and free.
May I see myself with the eyes of compassion.
May I be free from anxiety, worry, and fear.
May the Spirit guide and support me.
May I be loved, cared for, and nurtured.
May I be healed.

*Quiet, contemplative prayer happens when we are
still and open ourselves to Christ's Spirit working
secretly in us, when we heed the psalmist's plea:
"Be still and know that I am God." (Ps. 46:10)
These are times when we trustingly sink into God's
formless hands for cleansing, illumination, and
communion. Sometimes spontaneous sounds
and words come through us in such prayer, but
more often we are in a state of quiet appreciation,
simply hollowed out for God.*

Tilden Edwards, from his book *Living in the Presence* (p. 11)

Chapter Six: Meditation and Contemplative Prayer

Meditation and Contemplative Prayer

Centering Prayer

The Welcoming Prayer

Christian Meditation

The Jesus Prayer

The Yahweh Prayer

Mindfulness Meditation

Meditation and Contemplative Prayer

The term meditation is very broad and encompasses a number of different techniques and crosses many spiritual traditions. Whether the practice is from our friends to the East in the Buddhist and Hindu traditions or from the Western Christian contemplative prayer practices, the similarities seem apparent but can be very different in practice. The meditation practices like Centering Prayer, Transcendental Meditation, or the Buddhist practice called "Insight Meditation," are very different, but from the novice meditator's perspective, they probably seem very similar.

In her book, *Centering Prayer and Inner Awakening,* Cynthia Bourgeault explains the differences among the many meditation styles and practices. She explains:

> ... the various methodologies of meditation can be divided into three main groups: concentrative methods, awareness methods, and surrender methods. Centering Prayer belongs to this last (and least common) category. (p. 20)

> Concentrative methods ... rely on the principle of attention. The mind is given a simple task to focus its attention on, or more accurately, *in*. This might involve counting one's breaths ... or, most commonly, reciting a mantra either aloud or silently. (p. 20)

She goes on to discuss the second of the three, the awareness methods found in the Buddhist tradition:

> In awareness meditation, one aligns oneself with an inner observer and simply watches the play of energy as thoughts and emotions arise, take form, and dissipate.... The fruits of this type of meditation tend to be a laser-like clarity and a fierce, unshakeable *presence*. (pp. 20–21)

Finally, she describes the surrender method used in Centering Prayer from the Christian tradition:

> A surrender method is even simpler. One does not even watch or label the thought as it comes up.... As soon as it emerges into consciousness, one simply lets it go. The power of this form of meditation does not reside in a particular clarity of the mind or even in presence, but entirely in the gesture of release itself. Thomas Keating likes to characterize it as a prayer "not of attention, but of intention." (p. 21).

In the basic instruction of these three types of meditation techniques, you sit quietly and breathe normally. With a straight back and relaxed but intentional posture, you simply sit for twenty or thirty minutes. At that point, the three meditation styles use distinctly different approaches. In the following pages, I will introduce examples of the three styles to give you a choice of what might resonate with you. I encourage you to try each style. As I have said many times in this guidebook, try them, and if one resonates with you, pursue more information on the technique and the tradition from which it originates. For me, it was the Christian form of meditation called "Centering Prayer." The important thing is to experience a meditation practice in order to begin to understand and experience the silence and stillness that it brings to your prayer life.

I will leave you with one important idea as I introduce you to these different forms of meditation. This can be a life-changing experience, especially if you approach it with the idea that it could become a lifelong practice. Many have started a meditation practice and stopped only after a month or two. It will take time to truly develop a practice that is sustaining over time, but I assure you, it will be well worth it. It is hard for me to imagine that all those desert fathers and mothers, mystics and saints, and spiritual writers of the past (and present) were all wrong about the transformational qualities of sitting in silence in God's presence.

Centering Prayer

There is a well-known story about the beginnings of the Centering Prayer movement. Father Thomas Keating, a Cistercian monk who brought us this powerful prayer practice, was outside working with a fellow monk at the abbey. He noticed that every so often some young people would go by, headed up the road to some sort of spiritual center from one of the Eastern traditions that was gaining in popularity. Curious as to where they were going, he stopped a group of them and asked what was happening up the road. They told him they were going to learn how to meditate.

Later that day, he and his fellow monks discussed the encounter. They concluded meditation is something the monks have been doing for centuries in the monasteries, so why would it not be possible to teach our brothers and sisters in the Christian tradition our method of meditation? And the Centering Prayer movement began.

There are many stories like this one. Another well-known story came from a retreat Father Keating was giving in the early years of his teachings. After a thirty-minute sit, Father Keating was taking questions. A young nun raised her hand and in a frustrated voice said she was not sure she would ever master Centering Prayer. She lamented she had a thousand thoughts during the meditation and was not able to concentrate. Father Keating responded by pointing out to her how wonderful it was she had a thousand opportunities to come back to God.

There are numerous books available on Centering Prayer. I list several of them in the bibliography. My favorite is *Centering Prayer and Inner Awakening* by Cynthia Bourgeault, an Episcopal priest. Her explanations and instructions are clearly written and easy to follow. I am only providing you with an introduction to the practice. As with the other practices in the guidebook, I hope what I provide you will get you started. If the practice resonates with you, you can read more about it from such experts as Bourgeault, Keating, and others. Or even better, you can take a class from a certified teacher in your area. Go to the web site contemplativeoutreach.org to find a class near you.

Now let us begin. Find a place where you will not be disturbed and turn off all devices that have the potential to interrupt or distract you. Let your family members know you are not to be disturbed, pets included. Later, I will share a story of pets and prayer. Sit in a comfortable chair and keep your back as straight as possible with feet resting solidly on the floor. As a beginner, it is recommended that you spend fifteen or twenty minutes in the meditation. This will require you to have a way to time yourself. You can use a clock on the wall or a timer. The Contemplative Outreach staff provide a wonderful free app that you can download that provides a timer and a choice of chimes.

You will be using a prayer word or sacred word that you will repeat as a grounding or anchor to bring you back to your meditation as thoughts enter your mind. More on that in a minute. In choosing a sacred word, sit quietly and ask the Spirit for guidance. Some suggestions to get you started are such words as "Abba" or "Jesus" or "love" or "beloved" or any other word that comes to you. Ask the Holy Spirit to help you with this and trust the response you get. Once you have settled on a word, you will be using it from that point on, but it certainly can be changed. Preferably, however, not in the middle of your meditation.

Sit quietly and breathe evenly and relaxed. Close your eyes and, with intention, ask the Holy Spirit to be with you. In my practice, I begin by reciting a short prayer from Psalm 46, verse 10:

Be still and know that I am God.
Be still and know that I am.
Be still and know.
Be still.
Be.

Now begin to repeat the sacred word. When thoughts enter your mind and you become aware of them, gently let them go and return to the sacred word. In teaching this practice, Father Keating uses the metaphor of imagining that you are sitting on the bank of a river watching things go by. Treat these interrupting thoughts as the objects floating by on the river: boats, trash, people in canoes or kayaks, etc., and simply let them pass by without judgment and return to the sacred word.

The mind is very busy. The Buddhists call it "monkey mind." It is just part of the human condition, so do not let all of these thoughts coming at you discourage you. Simply recognize them, accept them, and then let them go and return to the sacred word. As I discussed earlier, Centering Prayer meditation practice is considered a surrendering method where the person uses the sacred word as an anchor to help release these thoughts as they enter your mind. It is not the same as using the word as a mantra repeated systematically, often with every breath, as in the concentrative methods.

At the end of the twenty-minute prayer period, sit quietly for a few moments. Many practitioners, when finished, say the *Our Father* as a way to bring them out of the meditation. In the beginning, one period of twenty minutes is recommended. This can be extended to thirty minutes and, ideally, one would want to eventually go to two twenty- to thirty-minute prayer periods a day.

I will not attempt to discuss all of the benefits of this prayer practice. You can find that in the books I have recommended. This description of Centering Prayer is designed simply as an introduction to what many believe to be a powerful and profound contemplative practice.

A few years ago, I was facilitating a men's contemplative prayer group that met at one of the men's homes. I noticed as I entered the home that first night the host had two small dogs. About five minutes into our first group experience with Centering Prayer, the dogs entered the room and began barking. Fortunately, after a few moments, the dogs stopped. At the end of the meditation, I looked down and one of the dogs was asleep at my feet. One of the men noted that he actually did not mind the barking interruption as it brought him back to the sacred word. I don't recommend this particular method to bring you back to the sacred word.

The Welcoming Prayer

The Welcoming Prayer originated from the work of Father Thomas Keating and the staff from Contemplative Outreach. Here I will attempt to give you an explanation of what the Welcoming Prayer is and an introduction to the practice. If you try the practice and it resonates with you, I strongly recommend you go to the web site of Contemplative Outreach and take an online class, or purchase the CD or written material.

I have introduced you to the practice of Centering Prayer. The Welcoming Prayer is a practice to do in addition to Centering Prayer and is defined as a companion practice. Many people struggle with meditation or Centering Prayer, because it can bring up unpleasant thoughts and emotions to the surface which, according to Father Keating, is not necessarily a bad thing. The problem is you need a strategy to work through those thoughts and feelings. The Welcoming Prayer is a practice that helps you focus on those feelings, recognize them for what they are, and then let them go with a series of statements, all with the guidance and support of the Holy Spirit.

It will be important for you to recognize the common thread running through the two prayer practices: the important process of letting go of your desire to control and then moving on. In Centering Prayer, the practice is to recognize thoughts as they arise, and simply let them go and return to your sacred word. With the Welcoming Prayer, you are verbalizing the letting go in a series of statements. Father Keating tells us you are changing the old negative tapes running in your head.

The actual practice or prayer only takes a few minutes of your time. I practice the Welcoming Prayer in the morning. It can also be done any time during the day. In fact, that is what is recommended. As an unpleasant feeling or emotion arises during your daily life encounters, pause for a moment and focus on the feeling. Try and sense where in your body you are feeling the emotion. Is your stomach tightening, are you feeling a rise in your body temperature, or do you feel muscle tension somewhere? Quietly and with intention say the word "welcome," inviting the Holy Spirit to be with you. While still focusing on the sensation, repeat the letting go sentences below to open the healing action of the Holy Spirit:

I let go of my desire for approval and affection ... Welcome
I let go of my desire for security and survival ... Welcome
I let go of my desire for power and control ... Welcome
I let go of my desire to change (any situation, person,
event, emotion) ... Welcome

In their booklet on the Welcoming Prayer, *Welcoming Prayer: The Contemplative Life Program*, the Contemplative Outreach staff explain the process of letting go this way:

Saying the "letting go" sentences gets to the root of obstacles in the unconscious — we consent to the dismantling of the exaggerated emotional programs for happiness that can't possibly work. (p. 30)

This practice of surrender is widely used in the spiritual teachings of all the mystics and saints and modern-day spiritual writers. It is also one of the main teachings in the twelve-step program. Just this week I was reading the words of Sister Joyce Rupp in her thought for the day in the *Living Faith: Daily Catholic Devotional*:

Who likes to get down on our bumbling knees and implore Holy Wisdom for guidance, pleading hints of "surrender," and who wants to totally give one's self in trust to this Unseen Leader? My inclination leans toward being in charge, figuring things out for myself. This part of self, "the ego," seeks to be chief and master, locking us in our small world of security and power.

My explanation of the Welcoming Prayer is designed only as a brief introduction to the practice. Spend some time with the sentences above as part of your prayer practice and discern if they resonate with you. If during the day you encounter a situation where you sense the Welcoming Prayer may be helpful, just repeat the words provided above, "I let go of my desire for ..." and then "Welcome," and so on. I also recommend a visit to the Contemplative Outreach website for a more comprehensive explanation.

Christian Meditation

Another form of meditation from the Christian tradition comes to us from a Benedictine monk from England, John Main OSB, (1926-1982). He brought the practice of Christian meditation practiced by the monks in the monastery to the outside world in the same way his contemporary, Father Thomas Keating, introduced us to Centering Prayer. In many ways, Christian Meditation and Centering Prayer are similar. There are, however, some differences that I will attempt to explain. Let me first give you the wonderful description of the experience of meditation by John Main from the book *Fully Alive: The Daily Path of Christian Meditation*. This book was edited by Laurence Freeman, founder of the World Community of Christian Meditation and a long-time student of Main's:

> What I would say to you, therefore, as we begin is: learn
> to say your mantra with a growing simplicity and humility.
> Learn to be content with the simplicity and the poverty of the
> one little word. Everything else, you let go of. Letting go of all
> your past and all your plans for the future you enter into the
> present moment, the moment where the *now* of God's infinite
> love is flowing in your mind and heart with a power greater
> than that of the mightiest river or waterfall in the world. All
> we have to do is enter in. The power of that great river of
> love, of that water welling up to eternal life, will sweep us
> beyond ourselves. We know not where. But what we do know
> is that by wholly opening ourselves to its power we will be
> swept into the mystery of God's infinite love. (pp. 5–6)

Some of what I will be sharing with you about the practice of Christian Meditation comes from a small book from Laurence Freeman titled: *Christian Meditation: Your Daily Practice*. Only sixty-three pages in length, it is full of good information about Christian Meditation and contemplative prayer in general.

As with Centering Prayer, find a place where you will not be disturbed. Turn off all devices that could interrupt or distract you. Find a comfortable chair, and sit with your back as straight as possible and your feet on the floor. Sit quietly and breathe easily and relax. Say a prayer to ground yourself and let the Spirit know your intention to be in God's presence. You will be sitting for about twenty minutes as a starting point, so it is suggested you have a way to time yourself. A timer or clock or watch will work. Eventually, it is recommended that the meditation be done twice a day, in the morning and evening.

The practice of Christian Meditation uses a mantra that is universal. It is the ancient Aramaic phrase "Maranatha," which translates as "Come, Lord or the "Lord comes." It is said in four syllables of equal length and continuously (Ma-ra-na-tha). One way of using the mantra is to say the first two syllables with the in breath and the last two as you exhale. As I explained in the introduction to this section on meditation, this meditation practice using a mantra is considered concentrative, relying on the principle of attention. Cynthia Bourgeault in her book, *Centering Prayer and Inner Awakening*, explains it this way:

> ... the mantra provides a touchstone for attention. Rather than allowing the mind to wander, it is anchored steadily and constantly in the simple repetition of the task. The mind stays alert and present while the deeper waters of one's being are refreshed in the numinous presence which the mantra itself invokes. (p. 20)

And Laurence Freeman in his book, *Christian Meditation: Your Daily Practice*, provides this explanation:

> Say [the mantra] without haste and without expecting anything to happen. Listen to the mantra with your whole being. Gently return to it whenever you get distracted. Be simple. Be faithful. (p. 20)

At the end of the twenty-minute meditation, you can recite a short prayer of gratitude. Sit quietly and reflect on the time in deep silence and presence. This often can be a good time to journal or read some spiritual material from a book of daily meditations. See the bibliography for some suggestions.

I want to leave you with some of the beautiful words from John Main and his writings from *Fully Alive: The Daily Path of Christian Meditation:*

> In meditating, we leave behind our own limited view of reality and, by paying full attention to what is, we begin to see everything bathed in that light, the light of truth which is the light of love. (p. 69)

> Without the attention of an attentive spirit, our religion and any pursuit of a spiritual path remain at the level of theory. (p. 63)

> ... it is important to understand that all significant growth starts from the interior. Essential personal growth begins in the deepest centre of our being and then grows outward. (p. 23)

> [When we meditate] remember only that God is. God is here. God is now. God is in my heart. God is love. The requirements are stillness, awareness, simplicity, commitment, discipline. Sit still. Say the word from beginning to the end. The mantra is the way. (p. 32)

The Jesus Prayer

The Jesus Prayer is an ancient prayer practice that goes back to the Desert Fathers and was continued most prevalently in the Eastern Orthodox Catholic Church. I have included it here in the meditation portion of the guidebook because that is the way it is most often used. The words of the Jesus Prayer contain a short phrase, often used as a mantra, "Lord Jesus Christ, have mercy on me, a sinner." These words are often modified slightly, as is the case, below, in a description of the Jesus Prayer by Martin Laird in his book on contemplation, *Into the Silent Land*:

> What is the Jesus Prayer? It is an ancient way of praying that disposes the one who prays to the open depths within by drawing to stillness the wandering mind that flits and skitters all over the place. Normally our attention finds it difficult to be still; it is forever chasing the myriad thoughts with the result that there is a great deal of chatter going on in our heads. The Jesus Prayer, indeed any contemplative discipline, tries to interrupt this chatter. Instead of allowing the attention to be stolen yet again by our inner chatter, our attention is given a short phrase or word to quietly repeat, such as the Jesus Prayer: "Lord Jesus Christ, Son of God, have mercy on me," or quite simply the word "Jesus." The use of a prayer word or phrase to recollect the obsessive dimensions of the mind reaches far back into the Christian tradition. (p. 48)

Using the Jesus Prayer as a mantra in meditation would be similar to the Christian Meditation technique or practice described earlier in this section. There are several ways one can say the prayer. I provide a few samples at the end of this section. Following the same process discussed in prior meditation techniques, find a comfortable place where you will not be disturbed. Turn off all devices that might distract you. Sit quietly with your back as straight as possible, breathe normally and relax your body. You might want to use the relaxation technique discussed in Chapter Two.

Close your eyes, and focus your attention on the present moment and being in God's presence. Begin repeating the Jesus Prayer in your mind. It can often work well if you repeat the first part of the phrase, "Lord Jesus Christ," on the in-breath and, "Have mercy on me, a sinner," on the exhale. Some people don't like the emphasis on the word sinner. In that case, use the phraseology mentioned above from Laird, "Lord Jesus Christ, Son of God, have mercy on me." Or you can say, "Have compassion for me,"

Continue repeating the phrase however you prefer for twenty to thirty minutes. As your mind wanders, and it will wander, come back to the phrase as you would in the other forms of meditation. In another section of Laird's book, he talks about the Desert Fathers when using the Jesus Prayer, and simply shortening the phrase to just saying "Jesus."

Several years ago I was watching a program about a group of Eastern Orthodox monks. It showed a young monk working away at a project in the monastery and repeating the Jesus Prayer over and over. It is practice they do as they work through the day. I would not expect anyone to take the practice to that extreme, but it does point out a way to use the prayer in other ways besides in meditation. You can say the prayer during the day when you have a few moments. Simply take a few deep breaths and repeat the prayer to yourself. Maybe you could repeat the prayer before going into a meeting at work, or just prior to making that difficult phone call or when the children have pushed you to your limit. I could give many more examples, but I think you can now see how you can use the prayer during your daily activities.

Here are some examples of some different ways to say the prayer:

Lord Jesus Christ, Son of God, have mercy on me.
Lord Jesus Christ, Son of God, have mercy on me, a sinner.
Lord Jesus Christ, Son of God, have compassion for me.
Jesus, have mercy on me.
Come Lord Jesus.
Jesus.

The Yahweh Prayer

The word Yahweh comes to us from the Jewish tradition and was their name for God. In this tradition, saying the name of God was considered unspeakable. It was formally not spoken at all. This is written about in Father Richard Rohr's book, *The Naked Now*. Father Rohr describes the connection of the word Yahweh to the idea of simply breathing:

> This unspeakability has long been recognized, but we now know it goes even deeper: formally the word was not spoken at all, but *breathed!* Many are convinced that its correct pronunciation is an attempt to replicate and imitate the very sound of inhalation and exhalation. The one thing we do every moment of our lives is therefore to speak the name of God. This makes it our first and our last word as we enter and leave the world. (pp. 25–26)

I have discussed the use of different words such as the Jesus Prayer and Maranatha in our meditation practices. In both cases, I suggested you could say the word or phrase as you inhale and exhale. In the Yahweh prayer, the very word Yahweh was used as a way to say God while actually breathing the word. That is to say, by our very breathing, we are speaking God's name. During a period of meditation, you can use the word Yahweh as it was used in the Hebrew tradition by simply breathing the word on the inhale and on the exhale.

Again, as in other meditation practices, find a place where you will not be disturbed and turn off all your devices that could potentially distract you. Sit quietly and relax your body and breathe normally. Bring your attention to the present moment and focus on being in God's presence. Close your eyes and begin a soft, rhythmic breathing. As you inhale repeat the first part of the word Yahweh *(YAH)* and as you exhale repeat the last syllable *(WEH): YAH WEH. YAH WEH.* Continue this for fifteen or twenty minutes as a meditation.

More from Father Rohr from *The Naked Now*:

> For some years now, I have taught this to contemplative groups in many countries, and it changes peoples faith and prayer lives in substantial ways. I remind people that there is no Islamic, Christian, or Jewish way of breathing. There is no American, African, or Asian way of breathing. There is no rich or poor way of breathing. The playing field is utterly leveled. The air of the earth is one and the same air, and this Divine wind "blows where it will" (John 3:8) — which appears to be everywhere. No one or no religion can control this Spirit. (p. 26)

Mindfulness Meditation

"drink your tea slowly"

A very powerful meditation practice that is becoming more popular in the west is the practice of mindfulness. Why present an eastern Buddhist practice in a guidebook about Christian prayer and contemplative practices? Because any practice or discipline that has the potential to deepen your spiritual life, regardless of the tradition, is vital to your goal of deepening your relationship with the Divine. Developing an awareness of the present moment brings us to that place where we will find God, in the silence and stillness. The great spiritual teacher and Jesuit priest Anthony de Mello spent much of his time teaching the idea of simply being awake, or the concept of awareness and being in the moment. He even wrote a book called *Awareness*. In the opening line of the first chapter of *Awareness,* you will find these words from de Mello:

> "Spirituality means waking up. Most people, even though they don't know it, are asleep." (p. 5)

In his last published work before he died, *The Way to Love,* he writes this about awareness:

> Holiness is not an achievement, it is a Grace. A Grace called Awareness, a grace called Looking, Observing,

Understanding. If you could only switch on the light of awareness and observe yourself and everything around you throughout the day, if you would see yourself reflected in the mirror of awareness the way you see yourself reflected in a looking glass, that is, accurately, clearly, exactly as it is without the slightest distortion or addition, and if you observed this reflection without any judgement or condemnation, you would experience all sorts of marvelous changes coming about in you. (pp. 193–194)

We have discussed how you can achieve this awareness in the Christian meditation practices. Another proven way you can achieve this awareness is through the practice of mindfulness meditation. Regardless of the origin of the practice, it is important to develop these prayer disciplines in order to strengthen this awareness. The goal is to choose some form of meditation that resonates with you and you feel comfortable doing. Work to develop the practice to the point that you are sitting for twenty or thirty minutes each day simply resting in God's presence.

A well-known practice from our Buddhist friends is "Vipassana," or Insight Meditation. In the March 2015 issue of the magazine *Shambala Sun*, the Zen master Thich Nhat Hanh, who helped introduce mindfulness practices to the west, described mindfulness meditation or insight meditation in this way (only the main points are presented here):

- *Set aside a room or corner that you can use just for sitting.*

- *The sound of a bell is a wonderful way to begin the sit. If you do not have a bell you can download a recording of the sound.*

- *When you sit keep your spine straight, while allowing your body to relax. Relax every muscle in your body, including the muscles in your face.*

- *Notice your breathing. As you breathe in, be aware that you are breathing in. As you breathe out, notice that you are breathing out. As soon as we pay attention to our breath, body, breath and mind come together. Every in-breath can bring joy; every out-breath can bring calm and relaxation. This is a good enough reason to sit.*

- *When you breathe mindfully and joyfully, don't worry about what your sitting looks like from the outside.*

- *It's wonderful to have a quiet place to sit in your home or workplace. But you can practice mindful sitting wherever you are. Use the time to nourish and heal yourself.*

- *If you sit regularly, it will become a habit. Consider daily sitting practice to be a kind of spiritual food. Don't deprive yourself and the world of it.*

Adapted from *How to Sit*, Thich Nhat Hanh, Parallax Press.

It is not possible to explain or describe mindfulness in any comprehensive way here. There is so much rich information out there about it. I have recommended this practice to several of the people I meet with in spiritual direction. Another author to consider is Tara Brach, especially her podcast on iTunes or on her website. And even though he doesn't refer to it as mindfulness, Father de Mello and his writings on awareness are very good.

I will leave you with this thought by Thich Naht Hahn from his classic book, *The Miracle of Mindfulness,* published in 1975.

Drink your tea slowly and reverently, as if it is the axis on which the whole earth revolves — slowly, evenly, without rushing toward the future. Live the actual moment. Only this actual moment is life. (p. 30)

An authentic practice life isn't about seeking peak experiences but rather touching the wonder of the ordinary. This is made clear in a conversation that the Buddha is said to have had with a prince. The prince asked, "What do you and your monastics practice every day?" The Buddha responded, "We sit, we walk, and we eat." The Prince said, "We also do these things everyday, so how are you different?" The Buddha responded, "When we sit, we know we are sitting. When we walk, we know we are walking. When we eat, we know we are eating."

From an article in *Shambala Sun Magazine*, by Brother Phap Hai, *Walking: Meditation in Motion.* July 2014 (p. 45)

Chapter Seven: Active Prayer and Contemplation

Contemplative Walking

Journaling

Composing Your Own Prayer

Contemplative Walking

Many people who have difficulty sitting still for very long can experience the powerful benefits of contemplative prayer by simply going for a walk. Walking meditation, or going for a prayer walk, can be a wonderful way to be with God. Can this be prayer? The answer, of course, is yes. Wherever one is, they are in God's presence. Think of how you enjoy a walk with a friend or spouse. For me, it always seems easier to talk as the thoughts and words just seem to flow. I am sure it is the relaxing nature of doing this physical activity. In our relationship with God, one can also feel like you are walking with a friend.

Taking a walk in nature as a contemplative practice is a walk with the intention of being present to your surroundings and, most importantly, present to God. God is always with us, but we often are not thinking about His presence. We are thinking about work or our family or some pressing issue. In the contemplative experience, we are praying with intention. It is about being awake to what God has to say to us. That requires paying attention. In her companion workbook to her book *Sacred Rhythms*, Ruth Haley Barton presents the "how to" of the spiritual practices discussed in *Sacred Rhythms*. She says this about taking what she calls a "prayer walk":

A prayer walk is a spiritual discipline, in that we consciously invite God to go with us, ask him to help us experience fully the extraordinary gift of being in our bodies, and (when we are able to take our walk outdoors) invite him to reveal something of himself through nature.

From *Sacred Rhythms: Spiritual Exercises that Nourish the Soul and Transform Your Life* (p. 89-90)

In this practice, find a place where you can be relaxed and enjoy the walk. There are many peaceful and quiet trails or parks you may be able to access. Many people, including myself, use the latest devices when they exercise. You are going to want to leave your step counters and timing devices at home. This is a spiritual exercise, not just a physical one. As you begin your walk, start to notice your surroundings. Feel your body and your breathing and the way your feet hit the earth and the natural swinging of your arms. Notice the natural in and out of your breathing as you would if you were sitting and meditating.

As with other contemplative practices, let the Spirit know your intention. Acknowledge the presence of the Divine and invite her along with you. If you have a particular issue you are working through, ask for support and insight and then listen in the quiet of the walk. Be open to whatever comes to you, and, most importantly, stay present in the moment. Walk without a particular goal or time in mind, just walk.

Be open to and aware of the natural setting around you. Allow your senses to open up, and listen to the sounds and be aware of the smells. It always seems for me that when I am really paying attention on my walks, I see more beauty. It may be a beautiful wildflower or some small critter that has decided to join me. On one of my walks, a monarch butterfly flew in front of me and stayed with me for several hundred feet. Something else I often notice on my walk is the beauty and grandeur of the trees. I live in northern Michigan, where there is no shortage of beautiful trees of all shapes and sizes, reaching toward the heavens. I am reminded of the beautiful poem from Rabindranath Tagore, poet and artist who died in 1941:

Silence my soul,
These trees are prayers.
I asked the tree, "Tell me about God,"
then it blossomed.

From *The Gitanjali*

When you end your walk, say a prayer of thanksgiving for the beauty around you and the companionship. Take note of the insights or something you may have noticed along the walk. If possible, you may want to jot it down in a journal.

Many of the thoughts and ideas for this presentation on walking in nature are from Ruth Haley Barton and her book and companion workbook, *Sacred Rhythms*. You will find these books listed in the bibliography.

Journaling

When reading a guidebook on prayer and contemplative practices, one might wonder why a writing exercise like journaling is included. I am including journaling because I believe it can, in fact, be prayer. Anytime one sits down with intention and the guidance and support of the Holy Spirit, it can be a beautiful form of prayer. Many people struggle with traditional prayer, and journaling can be a wonderful alternative practice to help those who are finding their prayer life to be dry and uninspired. I offer the following from spiritual teacher James Finley, member of the Center for Action and Contemplation (CAC) core faculty who spent time in training in his early years with Thomas Merton. This quote is taken from a CAC daily meditation:

> A contemplative practice is any act, habitually entered into
> with your whole heart, as a way of awakening, deepening,
> and sustaining a contemplative experience of the inherent
> holiness of the present moment. Your practice might be
> some form of meditation, such as sitting motionless in
> silence, attentive and awake to the abyss-like nature of each
> breath. Your practice might be simple, heartfelt prayer, slowly
> reading the scriptures, gardening, baking bread, writing
> or reading poetry, drawing or painting, or perhaps running
> or taking long, slow walks to no place in particular. (CAC
> website, August 5, 2017)

Several years ago I was meeting with someone in a spiritual direction session. With some frustration in his voice, he commented that his prayer life was like dry toast. It was certainly a powerful metaphor. After some discussion, we moved on. Later in our session, he said that he was writing again and was meeting with a writing club. He was quite enthused as he discussed his experience. I reminded him that earlier he described his prayer life as being like dry toast. I then took the opportunity to affirm his writing and told him if done with intention, his writing was a form of prayer. What he brought to the writing was what was in his heart, where all meaningful prayer originates. That was apparent from his passion and enthusiasm as he described his experience. We spent several sessions after that discussion talking about a short story he was working on, and the characters in the story, and how it could all be related to his spiritual journey.

The technique of journaling needs little explanation. There are many different types of journals that you can find at any bookstore or online. The idea behind journaling is to be open and spontaneous as you write. Sit quietly and ask the Spirit to be with you. One technique is to simply sit and write whatever comes to mind, expressing your deepest feelings about an issue or problem you are working through. You can begin by writing the problem in the form of a question at the top of the page. Then simply reflect on the question and start writing whatever comes to mind. Journaling is a very effective way to go deeper in your prayer practice and give it more depth.

In an earlier prayer practice, I introduced Lectio Divina or "sacred reading." Journaling can be a great addition to the Lectio experience. After going through the four steps of Lectio, sit with your journal and write down your thoughts about the reading. Consider how the scripture text spoke to you. Reflect on what meaning the reading may have for your life at that moment. The same can be done using the Examen practice described earlier. After your reflection on the day's events, you can put them down in writing in your journal. This can be especially helpful if the day presented a particularly meaningful event or encounter.

Another time that can be fruitful for journaling is after a spiritual direction session. You can write down any significant insight you and your director may have uncovered. Journaling after a Sunday church service or other meaningful religious service can be a way to reflect and deepen that experience. Additionally, time spent journaling while attending a retreat can help deepen the retreat experience. This time is designed to be quiet and reflective, an ideal circumstance where journaling works well. Prayer and contemplation is about deepening your relationship with God. The practice of journaling is one very profound way to do that. As with other forms of prayer, it does not have to be done on a daily basis. Journal when you feel the time is right. Simply try it for a few weeks and see if it becomes a meaningful practice as part of your prayer life.

Composing Your Own Prayer

Nine years ago, I was in my first year of my spiritual direction formation program. One of the first books we read was *Fire and Love: Encountering the Holy Spirit,* by Donald Goergen, OP. At the end of each chapter, Father Goergen provided the reader with a beautiful prayer to the Holy Spirit. I was very taken with this and truly enjoyed reading the next new prayer at the end of each chapter. I particularly liked one of the prayers so I copied it and taped it to a three-inch by five-inch card. I began a nine-year daily recitation of that prayer every morning during my prayer time. It did not take long before I had it memorized.

One morning in class, during the time we were studying the Goergen book, the facilitator asked all of us to spend a few minutes writing our own prayer to the Holy Spirit. For me it was the start of long and amazing journey of prayer composition. I am sure if someone were to ask me what my hobbies were and I said, "Oh I really enjoy writing prayers," I am not sure what the reaction would be. I will admit I often borrow some of the words of some of the great prayer composers and adapt their words to my prayers. I always give them credit. Thank you, Sister Joyce Rupp, Father Thomas Merton, Father Donald Goergen, Sister Joan Chittister, Father Richard Rohr, and the wonderful words of the Irish Jesuits, just to name a few. I have provided a number of my favorite prayers in the back of the Guidebook. Some I authored, some are written by others.

I suggest simply sitting down with a journal or a pad of paper and start writing. Always start with a short prayer to the Holy Spirit asking for guidance and support. Writing your own prayer can be done in the same way. If there is someone in your life who needs a prayer — a family member, a friend or relative, or someone at work — write them a prayer. If there is someone with whom you are struggling, it can be a wonderful exercise to write a prayer for them. Whether you share the prayer with the person is your choice. I sometimes will ask a directee in a spiritual direction session who has just described a long list of grievances against someone, "What is your prayer for them?" The most common reaction is a startled look, then a moment of reflective pause, and then they are usually able to spontaneously recite a prayer of their own for that person.

One technique I use is to adapt something that was in narrative form I liked and put the words into the form of a prayer. One of my favorite prayers from Sister Joyce Rupp came from her web site. It was a prayer she wrote that she adapted from Psalm 139. It can be found in the back of this guidebook. We have been reading and reciting the prayers of others for all of our prayer life. Maybe it is time to author our own prayer. Simply open your heart and put to paper what it is you want to say to God for yourself or for someone else.

On the next page is the prayer to the Holy Spirit that I composed spontaneously while sitting in a classroom nine years ago. I offer it to you now as an example of what can happen when you simply open up and write from your heart.

Holy One, Help Me See Where You Are

Holy One, help me see where you are.
Are you here in my heart?
Help me find you, know you, and give me
the courage to trust you.
Divine One come upon me and lift me up,
open my heart to your grace.
Show me the infinite possibilities of love
that exist with in me.
Indwelling, you are at the core of my being,
help me to know always that you are there.
Help me to strengthen my inner life.
Bring me down and bring me home.
Allow the descent and protect me in that journey.
Be my guide, show me the way O Divine Friend,
and be by my side always.
Help me see what it is that I need to see and grow
in my love for all creation.
Bless us all and move us always toward your Divine love.

Final Thoughts

It is an honor and a privilege to write this guidebook, and to present some of the many prayer options that are available for the seeker to use on his or her journey. As I wrote in the beginning of the guidebook, my purpose is to introduce the reader to the many prayer and contemplative practices available, and to give you a starting point. If, after trying some of the practices, one of them resonates with you, work with it for a while. If, after spending some time with the practice, you decide it is something you want to pursue and study in more depth, refer to the bibliography or the list I have provided of suggested readings. There you will find many wonderful books by the experts in the world of prayer and contemplative practices. There is so much rich information out there for you to consider.

Some of the prayer practices presented in the guidebook may leave you wondering if this is an actual prayer at all. One of the goals of presenting so many different possibilities is to expand your understanding of the many kinds of prayer practices available to you. It is my hope that by presenting a wide range of possibilities, it will help you realize there are many powerful ways to experience the Holy One on your spiritual journey.

It is important to go slowly and thoughtfully as you further develop your prayer life. Have faith that the Holy Spirit is always with you, and desires to help and guide you along the way. It sometimes can feel like hard work to stick with something, but as you work at it you will begin to see the fruits of your prayer time and how it affects the rest of your life. It will be worth the effort. As I often remind people in my spiritual-direction practice, what happens in those times of deep reflection, contemplation, and meditation goes with you as you go out into the world of family and work. The fruits of spirit developed in your prayer practice will become a part of your life. As the last line from the prayer *Great Teacher* by Sister Joyce Rupp says, "As I go forth from my prayer, may I reflect the radiance of your goodness." (p. 120)

Another question that may be of concern for some is whether some of the practices presented in the guidebook can be considered Christian. An example is the Buddhist practices of metta and mindfulness included in the guidebook. In response, I would like to offer a quote from Tilden Edwards, an Episcopal priest and co-founder of the Shalem Institute in Washington, DC. In one of his many books on Christian contemplation, *Living in the Presence: Spiritual Exercises to Open Our Lives to the Awareness of God,* he offers this in his discussion of body prayer to those who are troubled by mixing Christian prayer practices and practices from other traditions:

> In the wider ecumenism of the Spirit being opened for us today, we need to humbly accept the learnings of particular Eastern religions in relation to the body now available to us. What makes a particular practice Christian is not its source, but its *intent*. If our intent in assuming particular bodily practice is to deepen our awareness in Christ, then it is Christian. If this is not our intent, then even the reading of Scripture loses its authenticity. (p. 18)

We began with the title: "Guarding the Heart: A Guidebook of Contemplative Prayer Practices." We end with these final words from Tilden Edwards as he quotes from one of the Desert Fathers, St. Sarephim of Sarov:

> If the fundamental spiritual discipline is prayer, opening to God, then the fundamental discipline of prayer is turning to our heart and inviting a sustained mutual presence. Sustaining this presence classically is called "guarding the heart." To paraphrase St. Seraphim of Sarov: "One must

constantly guard the heart. The heart cannot live unless it is full of that living water which boils in the heat of the divine fire. When this is poured out, the heart grows cold and becomes like an icicle."

From *Living in the Presence: Spiritual Exercises to Open Our Lives to the Awareness of God*. Tilden Edwards (pp. 12–13)

May you be blessed, always guard your heart, and always keep your barrel full.

Prayers

Prayers from Thomas Merton

My Lord God, I have no idea where I am going.
I do not see the road ahead of me.
I cannot know for certain where it will end.
Nor do I really know myself, and the fact
that I think I am following your will does not mean
that I am actually doing so. But I believe that
the desire to please you does in fact please you.
And I hope I have that desire in all that I am doing.
I hope that I will never do anything apart from that desire.
And I know that if I do this you will lead me
by the right road though I may know nothing about it.
Therefore I will trust you always though I may seem
to be lost and in the shadow of death.
I will not fear, for you are ever with me, and
you will never leave me to face my perils alone.

Amen

Dear God,
I have much to learn. Continue,
in your mysterious wisdom,
to send teachers into my life,
no matter how young or old,
who will teach me compassion,
kindness, gentleness, humility, and patience.
I am a ready student:
Let my teachers come.

Amen

Let me seek, then, the gift of silence, and
poverty, and solitude, where everything
I touch is turned into a prayer:
where the sky is my prayer, the birds are my
prayer, the wind in the trees is my prayer, for
God is all in all.

Amen

Prayers from Joyce Rupp

An Advent Prayer

Holy One, awaken my heart, quiet my mind,
open the door of my being to perceive your presence.
Settle what stirs endlessly within me.
Quiet the voice of haste and hurry.
Awaken my inner senses to recognize
your love hiding beneath the frenzy.
Enfold me in your attentiveness.
Wrap a mantle of mindfulness around every
part of my days. I want to welcome you with joy
and focus on your dwelling place.

Amen

Prayer to the Holy Spirit

*Come, Holy Spirit, help me replace the busyness of my
life with a simpler lifestyle, so I will focus on the essential
things in my life and allow time for others.*

*Nourish my ability to understand and appreciate myself.
Keep me from being too self-oriented and unmindful
of others' needs.*

*Fill me with trust of your consoling presence.
Calm me when I am anxious and troubled.*

*Help me to have the courage to empty myself
of anything that does not contribute to the
transformation of this world.*

*Continue to create a deep hunger for you within me.
Feed me with "the finest wheat" of your joy, peace, and
love. Replenish my weary spirit with an enthusiasm and
energy and that comes from surrendering my life to you.*

*Be my wisdom as I search for meaning in a world fraught
with pain, suffering, hostility and division. Keep me
hungry for you, Source of Life, so that I will always
ache and yearn for you.*

Amen

Interpretation of Psalm 139

Holy One, you created me in my mother's womb.
You know the core goodness residing within me.
You also know my propensity for self-orientation.
You see how I want others to meet my expectations.

You know the thoughts and feelings that run rampant
when I encounter someone whose behavior I resist.
If I say, "Surely I can get this person to be as I want,"
nudge me insistently with your grace-filled message:
"Leave the other person's transformation alone.
Tend to your aspects that need to be changed."

In this new year, guide me to a clearer awareness.
Lead me to move beyond a wish to transform others.
Focus my attention on how I approach what I resist.
May I become more alert and accepting of the reality
that the only person I can set about changing is myself.

Trusted Guide,

You are my mentor, my inspiration, my Home
of good choices and decisions.

You help me to search with confidence as I find
my way to inner peace.

Please gather your wisdom around me. Guide me carefully
as I make choices about how to use my energy positively.

Place your discerning touch on my mind
so that I will think clearly.

Place your loving fingers on my heart so I will be
more fully attentive to what is really of value.

Teach me how to hear your voice, to be aware
of what is in my mind and heart,
to attend to your wisdom in those around me,
to acknowledge my intuition and ponder my dreams,
to listen to the earth and all of life for in each piece
of my existence you are guiding me.

Guide of my life,
thank you for all you have given to me. Reveal
my spiritual path and direct me in the living of it.
Lead me to inner peace and oneness with you.

Amen

*When my heart slowly sinks
into a sense of unhappiness, and
when my mind whispers
about could, should and ought, and
when the voice of my false self, impatient
with the way people are, or are not,
and with the way I am, or am not,
please help me let all of that go.
Show me the way to step aside and
go to my inner dwelling place. The place
where your Divine light flames with
ceaseless love. Place me in the center of
that Love untouched by the demands
of my ego.*

*Lead me past all that hinders kindheartedness
from glowing steadily in my life.
Move me into that home of transformation,
into that grace-filled, spacious place.
Restore me, and renew me, and regenerate me.
Guide me as I go forth with hope,
to start again with less controlled expectation
and more peaceful receptivity
in the container of my mind and heart.*

*Give me the strength and the courage to
show compassion for the weak, the hardened,
the wounded, the burdened, the pained;
for each and every one
bears the reflection of my self,
my own glimpse of all that is yet to be purified
in the golden sphere of Your Divine love.*

Adapted from the words of Sister Joyce Rupp

Great Teacher

Great Teacher,
You draw me to your heart.
You reach me with your love.
You inspire me with your message,
and then you send me out to others.
May I love well.
As I go forth from my prayer,
may I reflect the radiance your goodness.

Amen

The Prayers of the Irish Jesuits
and other Celtic Prayers

Lord, may your Spirit guide us to seek

your loving presence more and more.

For it is there we find rest from this busy world.

And in this loving presence, we unwind this past day,

starting from now and looking back, moment by moment.

We gather in all the goodness and light, in gratitude.

We attend to the shadows and what they say to us,

seeking healing, courage and forgiveness. Amen

Adapted from the words of the Irish Jesuits, *Sacred Space, The Prayer Book, 2017*

Dear God, as we weave our way through life,
help us to discern what it is You want us to see.
Show us how we can reach to the heavens in our
daily communion with our brothers and sisters.
Help us to learn from our experience of life
what helps us live lovingly.

Adapted from the words of the Irish Jesuits, *Sacred Space,*
The Prayer Book, 2016

As I Sit Here

*As I sit here, I dwell for a moment on Your life-giving
presence, right here, right now. The beating of my heart,
the ebb and flow of my breathing and the movement of
my mind are all signs of Your ongoing presence within me.*

*As I sit here, I pause for a moment and become aware
of your presence within me. I remind myself that there
are things you have to teach me yet, and I ask for
the grace to hear them and let them change me.*

*As I sit here, I feel Your presence breathing life into me
and everything around me. Please help me to rise
above the noise, the noise that separates, the noise
that isolates, and to listen to your loving voice saying
"Come to me you who are overburdened and I will
give you rest, for I am gentle and humble of heart."
As I sit here, take me to the place where I know
You are, deep in the stillness.*

Amen

Adapted from the words of the Irish Jesuits and *Sacred Space,
The Prayer Book, 2016*

A Celtic Prayer

In the silence of our hearts or in spoken words
let us give thanks for the gifts of this day
and pray for the life of the world ...

(here brief prayers may be offered)

In the rising of the sun and its setting,
In the whiteness of the moon and its seasons,
In the infinity of space and its shining stars,
You are God and we bless You.
May we know the harmony of heaven
in the relationships of earth
and may we know the expanse of its mystery within us.

From *Celtic Treasure: Daily Scriptures and Prayers*
by J. Philip Newell

Celtic Metta Prayer

May our hearts be open to Spirit.
May we feel God's presence in our lives.
May we have forgiveness in our hearts.
May our fears yield our deepest tranquilities.

May all that is unlived in us blossom into a future
Graced with love.
May we be at peace in our heart.

Blessing

Bless to us, O God,
the moon that is above us,
the earth that is beneath us,
the friends who are around us,
Your image deep within us, Amen

From *The Iona Abbey Worship Book* (p.134)

We stumble on the journey, Oh God.
We lose heart along the way.
We forget your promises and blame one another.
Refresh us with the springs of your spirit in our souls
and open our senses to your guiding presence
that we may be part of the world's healing this day,
that we may be part of the world's healing.

From *Celtic Treasure: Daily Scriptures and Prayers*
by J. Phillip Newell.

Prayers from Richard Rohr and the CAC

God of life, bless our days.

Keep us alive and in love and keep us listening.

Keep us growing, Mother-God.

Keep drawing us closer to You.

*Help our words, Father-God, not get in the way of
Your Spirit.*

*Help the words we use not become too many
or too confusing.*

*Our faith, Holy One, is in You and not
in any words or teachings.*

*We just want those words to open us up to You
and to your Spirit among us.*

*Help us not to be afraid of Jesus,
the companion You have given us*

*for our journey towards You.
As St. Bernard prayed, "Jesus, Our Lord,
You are honey in our mouth. You are music in our ear.
You are a leap of joy in our heart."*

Amen

Let me be present in the now.

*It's all we have and it's where God will always
speak to me.*

*The now holds everything, rejects nothing and,
therefore, can receive God, too.*

*Help me to be present to the place I am most afraid of,
because it always feels empty, it always feels boring,
it always feels like it is not enough.*

*Help me find some space within that I don't try to fill
with ideas or opinions.*

*Help me to create inner space,
because you always show yourself best when
I am hungry and empty.*

*Keep me out of the way,
so there is always room enough for you.*

Amen

Most high, glorious God, enlighten
the darkness of my heart.

Give me true faith, certain hope, perfect charity,
sense and knowledge, Lord, that I may carry out
Your holy and true command.

And for as long as space endures and for as long
as living beings remain, until then may I, too, be able
to dispel the misery of the world.

Adapted from the words of St. Frances and the Dalai Lama

Prayer From Henri Nouwen

Dear God,

Speak gently in my silence.

When the loud outer noises of my surroundings
and the loud inner noises of my fears
keep pulling me away from you,
help me to trust that you are still there
even when I am unable to hear You.

Give me the ears to listen to Your small soft voice saying:

"Come to me, you who are overburdened,
and I will give you rest... for I am gentle and humble
of heart." (Matt. 11:28-30)

Let that loving voice be my guide.

Amen

St. Paul's Prayer to the Ephesians
Chapter 3, Verses 14 through 19

I bow my knees before the Father, from whom
every family in heaven and on earth takes its name.
I pray that, according to the riches of God's glory,
God may grant that we may be strengthened in
our inner being with power through the Spirit, and
that Christ may dwell in our hearts through faith,
as we are being rooted and grounded in Love.

I pray that we may have the power to comprehend,
with all the saints, what is the breadth and length
and height and depth, and to know the love of Christ
that surpasses knowledge, so that we may be filled
with all the fullness of God.

Dear God,

I know that in any moment, no matter how lost I feel,
I can take refuge in Your presence and love.
I need only pause, breathe, and be open to the experience.
In that wakeful openness, I come home to the peace
and freedom of my naked awareness and the
Divine within me.

I am humbled and I am grateful.

Amen

Adapted from Tara Brach, Buddhist Teacher

Suggested Readings on Contemplative Prayer

Sacred Rhythms: Arranging Our Lives for Spiritual Transformation, Ruth Haley Barton. A spiritual director trained at the Shalem Institute, Barton describes the many important spiritual disciplines to aid the seeker on their journey.

Sacred Rhythms: Spiritual Practices that Nourish Your Soul and Transform Your Life, Ruth Haley Barton. This is a workbook that describes the "how to" for the practices discussed in her book, *Sacred Rhythms*.

Opening to God: Lectio Divina and Life as Prayer, David G. Benner. A beautiful explanation of Lectio Divina and Centering Prayer and developing a deeper prayer life.

The Wisdom Jesus: Transforming Heart and Mind, Cynthia Bourgeault. Bourgeault is an Episcopal priest who studied with Basil Pennington. In the last part of the book, she describes the various types of contemplative prayer, including a nice description of Centering Prayer.

Centering Prayer and Inner Awakening, Cynthia Bourgeault. A comprehensive discussion of Centering Prayer. This is a must-read if you are considering this prayer practice.

Prayer in the Cave of the Heart: The Universal Call to Contemplation, Cyprian Consiglio. Father Consiglio is a monk who studied in India. He does a wonderful job of tying together the concepts of contemplation with the Eastern religious practices of meditation.

Sadhana, a Way to God: Christian Exercises in Eastern Form, Anthony de Mello, S.J. Father de Mello was a Jesuit priest who studied in India and brings those Eastern influences to the teachings of St. Ignatius. He provides many powerful guided meditations.

Living in the Presence: Spiritual Exercises to Open Our Lives to the Awareness of God, Tilden Edwards. Edwards is the co-founder of the Shalem Institute in Washington, DC. He is one of the leading teachers and writers on Contemplative Prayer.

Christian Meditation: Experiencing the Presence of God, James Finley. Finley studied under Thomas Merton. Anything by Finley is worth reading.

The Examen Prayer: Ignatian Wisdom for Our Lives Today, Timothy M. Gallagher, O.M.V. This book provides a comprehensive description of the *Prayer of Examen* from St. Ignatius.

Meditation and Contemplation: An Ignatian Guide to Prayer and Scripture, Timothy Gallagher, O.M.V. Father Gallagher has written extensively on Ignatian Spirituality. He has a very readable style and provides a lot of good information on developing a deeper prayer life.

The Cloud of Unknowing, edited by William Johnston. The author of this book is unknown. A very powerful book and a must-read for anyone interested in developing a deeper prayer life. Best to read in small bits.

Invitation to Love: The Way of Christian Contemplation, Thomas Keating. Father Keating is one of the leading proponents of Centering Prayer and has written much on the topic. He also has a web site. This is an excellent how-to guide to Centering Prayer.

A Sunlit Absence: Silence, Awareness, and Contemplation, Martin Laird, O.S.J. There is much thought and depth in this book. It is a must-read if your goal is to go deeper in your practice.

New Seeds of Contemplation, Thomas Merton. This is a classic and a must-read for anyone interested in a contemplative prayer life. Best to read it slowly, a few pages a day.

Blessed Relief: What Christians Can Learn from Buddhists about Suffering, Gordon Peerman. An Episcopal priest, Peerman does a wonderful job of merging east and west in contemplative practices. There are good suggestions at the end of each chapter on prayer practices.

Finding Grace at the Center: The Beginning of Centering Prayer, Basil Pennington and Thomas Keating. A short book of only 100 pages, but full of good information about Centering Prayer.

Centered Living: The Way of Centering Prayer, Basil Pennington. Father Pennington partnered with Father Keating in founding the Centering Prayer Movement. He is a very good writer and an obvious expert on the concepts of Centering Prayer.

Everything Belongs: The Gift of Contemplative Prayer, Father Richard Rohr. Father Richard is a Franciscan priest and founder of the *Center for Action and Contemplation*. He has written extensively on all aspects of spirituality. Any book by Rohr will challenge you.

Prayer, Joyce Rupp. A wonderful book on prayer and developing a daily prayer life. In my opinion, anything by Joyce Rupp is worth reading.

Bibliography

Adams, Caroline Joy. *A Woman of Wisdom: Honoring and Celebrating Who We Are.* Celestial Arts, 1999

Barton, Ruth Haley. *Sacred Rhythms: Arranging Our Lives for Spiritual Transformation.* IVP Press, 2006

Barton, Ruth Haley. *Sacred Rhythms: Spiritual Practices that Nourish Your Soul and Transform Your Life.* Zondervan, 2011

Benner, David G. *Opening to God: Lectio Divina and Life as Prayer.* IVP Books, 2010

The Bible. *The New American Bible. The New Catholic Translation.* Thomas Nelson, Inc., 1987

Bourgeault, Cynthia. *The Wisdom Jesus: Transforming Heart and Mind-A New Perspective on Christ and his Message.* Shambala, 2008

Bourgeault, Cynthia. *Centering Prayer and Inner Awakening.* Cowley Publications, 2004

Brantley, Mary, and Tesilya Hanauer. *The Gift of Loving Kindness.* New Harbinger Publications, 2008

De Caussade, Jean-Pierre, S.J. *Abandonment to Divine Providence: How to Fulfill Your Daily Duties with God Given Purpose.* Saint Benedict Press Classics, 2008

de Mello, Anthony, S.J. *Awareness: The Perils and Opportunities of Reality.* Image Books, 1990

de Mello, Anthony, S.J. *Sadhana, a Way to God: Christian Exercises in Eastern Form.* Image Books, 1978

de Mello, Anthony, S.J. *The Way to Love: The Last Meditations of Anthonyd.* Image Books Doubleday, 1991

Edwards, Tilden. *Living in the Presence: Spiritual Exercises to Open Our Lives to the Awareness of God.* HarperOne, 1994

Fleming, David, S.J. *Draw Me Into Your Friendship: The Spiritual Exercises, A Literal Translation and Contemporary Reading.* The Institute of Jesuit Sources, 1996

Freeman, Laurence, O.S.B. *Christian Meditation: Your Daily Practice.* Novalis, Reprint 2014

Gallagher, Timothy, O.M.V. *The Examen Prayer: Ignatian Wisdom for Our Lives Today.* The Crossroad Publishing Company, 1996

Hai, Brother Phap. *Walking: Meditation in Motion.* Shambala Sun Magazine, July 2014. Wisdom Publications.

The Iona Community. *Iona Abbey Worship Book.* Wild Goose Publications, 2001

The Irish Jesuits. *Sacred Space: The Prayer Book, 2017.* Loyola Press, 2016

Laird, Martin, O.S.A. *A Sunlit Absence: Silence, Awareness, and Contemplation.* Oxford University Press, 2011

Laird, Martin, O.S.A. *Into the Silent Land: A Guide to the Christian Practice of Contemplation.* Oxford University Press, 2006

Living Faith: Daily Catholic Devotional. October, November December 2016. Ignatius Press.

Main, John. *Fully Alive: The Daily Path of Christian Meditation.* Laurence Freeman, Editor. Orbis Books, 2011

Martin, James, S.J. *The Jesuit Guide to (Almost) Everything: A Spirituality for Real Life.* HarperOne, 2012

Merton, Thomas. *Conjectures of a Guilty Bystander.* Image Books/ Doubleday Religion, 1965

Merton, Thomas. *New Seeds of Contemplation.* Shambala, 2003

Merton, Thomas. *Thoughts in Solitude.* Farrar, Straus and Giroux, 1958

Muldoon, Tim, Ph.D. *The Ignatian Workout: Daily Spiritual Exercises for a Healthy Faith.* Loyola Press, 2004

Newell, J. Phillip. *Celtic Treasures: Daily Scriptures and Prayers.* William B. Eerdmans Publishing Company, 2005

Nichtern, Ethan. *Tonglen: In with the Bad, Out with the Good.* Shambala Sun, July 2014

Nouwen, Henri J. M. *Clowning in Rome: Reflections on Solitude, Celibacy, Prayer, and Contemplation.* Image Books, 1979

Nouwen, Henri. *With Open Hands.* Ave Maria Press

Rohr, Richrd. *Daily Meditations,* Center For Action and Contemplation. Web (CAC.org)

Rohr, Richard. *The Naked Now: Learning to See as the Mystics See.* The Crossroad Publishing Company, 2009

Rohr, Richard. *Yes, and . . . : Daily Meditations. Franciscan Media, 2013*

Rupp, Joyce. *Prayer.* Orbis Books, 2008

Salzberg, Sharon. *Loving-Kindness: The Revolutionary Art of Happiness.* Shambala, 1995

Thich Nhat Hanh. *The Miracle of Mindfulness: A Manual on Meditation.* Beacon Press, 1975

Thich Nhat Hanh. *How to Sit.* Shambala Sun Magazine, March 2014. Wisdom Publications

Welcoming Prayer. The Contemplative Life Program. Contemplative Outreach Media Center, 2006

Mike has been practicing Spiritual Direction for nine years and has been leading Contemplative Prayer groups over the last several years. He was certified in spiritual direction after completing a three-year Spiritual Formation program at the Dominican Center at Marywood in Grand Rapids, Michigan. He is currently participating in a spiritual formation program with the Shalem Institute in Washington, D. C., working towards a certification in contemplative prayer group leadership and retreat leadership. Mike retired in 2007 after 35 years with Michigan Department of Social Services where he worked as a social worker and administrator. He resides in Northern Michigan.

Made in the USA
Lexington, KY
20 February 2018